THE HISTORY OF THE GREEN BAY PACKERS

LOMBARDI'S DESTINY

PART THREE

FIRST EDITION

LARRY D. NAMES

LARANMARK PRESS/
EAGAN HILL PUBLISHERS
RIO, WISCONSIN
USA

LOMBARDI'S DESTINY – PART THREE

THE HISTORY OF THE GREEN BAY PACKERS

ISBN-13: 978-0-910937-90-0

Library of Congress Control Number: 2025917554

Cover photo:
The Green Bay Packers defeated the Cleveland Browns 23-12 in the NFL Championship Game, held on January 2, 1966. This was the last NFL Championship before the introduction of the Super Bowl. That is #5 Paul Hornung carrying the ball.

Photographs courtesy of Jeff Everson Collection, Larry Names Collection & many thanks to Green Bay Packers Hall of Fame.

www.larrynames.com

To Cliff Crystl

Thanks for making

me dig deeper.

Table of Contents

Acknowledgements

I would like to thank Wayne Mausser and Jeff Everson for their contributions to the production of this book.

Many thanks to Rick Shaq" Goldstein for his excellent suggestions for making the statistics more readable.

§ § §

Foreword

by
Wayne Mausser

More kudos for Larry Names. The History of the Green Bay Packers-Lombardi's Destiny, Part 3 covers the 1965 Packers championship season and return to glory in minute detail.

Larry Names has not only captured Vince Lombardi's magnetism and desire to win and inspiration for his players, but it also details his drive to motivate a team that suffered injuries to key players to achieve their best.

After the NFL Championship's in 1963 and 1964, which were won by the Bears and Browns respectively, Lombardi, the motivator was himself motivated and would do what it took to coach his team back to championship glory.

In 1963 the Packers went 11-2-1 in the Western Conference, finishing behind the eventual champion, Chicago Bears. Chicago won both of its games against Green Bay, 10-3 in their first meeting at Green Bay and 26-7 in their second game on November 17th at Wrigley Field. The Bears would go on to beat the New York Giants and aging quarterback Y.A. Tittle, 14-10, at Wrigley.

In 1964 the Packers finished a disappointing 8-5-1, good for second place in the NFL Western Conference. They went on to compete in the NFL Playoff Bowl on January 2nd, 1965, losing, 24-17, to the St. Louis Cardinals at the Orange Bowl in Miami. The game was played before a record crowd of 56,218. The Cleveland Browns would go on to win the Championship, shutting out the Baltimore Colts, 27-0.

So again, not winning in those two seasons set the stage for a comeback in 1965, back to the glory years of 1961 and 1962 when the team won back-to-back Championships.

In 1965 the Coach and GM had a good nucleus of returning veteran offensive players, like Bart Starr, Paul Hornung, Jim Taylor, and backup quarterback Zeke Bratkowski, who would start and win several games in the place of the often-injured Starr. There were also talented wide receivers in the newly acquired Carroll Dale, along with veterans Boyd Dowler and Max McGee. The tight ends were Marv Flemming and Bill Anderson.

The offensive line was solid with tackle Forrest Gregg, guards Jerry Kramer and Fuzzy Thurston, and Ken Bowman and Bill Curry, sharing the center position. The defense was once again a force to be reckoned with, with the likes of lineman Willie Davis, who was a standout player known for his pass rushing skills, and middle linebacker Ray Nitschke, who epitomized the ferocity of his coach, with a desire to not only to win, but to dominate with tough, physical play. It also featured starting left linebacker Dave Robinson and a ball hawking defensive secondary, led by the speedy Willie Wood, Herb Adderley, Bob Jeter, and Hank Gremminger. Other key contributors in the secondary were Doug Hart and Tom Brown. Adderly and Moore were the primary kickoff and punt return specialists. Don Chandler was brought in, not only as the team's punter but also doubled as the placekicker, in place of Hornung. Chandler would kick a memorable 22-yard field goal in the 1965 Western Conference Playoff game against the Baltimore Colts, which tied the score at 10-10. The Packers would eventually win in overtime on another Chandler three-pointer to win, 13-10. They would later beat the Cleveland Browns and the great running back Jim Brown, 23-12, and bring the NFL Championship back to Green Bay.

As you can see, Green Bay had a lot of great talent on both sides of the ball, but the key behind it all was the looming and dominating presence of their head coach, Vince Lombardi. He was honest with his players and drove them hard in practice-as usual. They not only were playing for their jobs, but they also shared the drive Lombardi displayed, which was to play hard, disciplined football, making few mental mistakes and forcing turnovers when the opportunity came and then taking advantage of them. In the process, Lombardi was able to gain that important trust from his players.

Larry Names also delves painstakingly into the fascinating history of the Green Bay Packers, starting with Curly Lambeau and his contributions to the Packers and the city of Green Bay. His thorough research into the early years of the team sets the stage for Lombardi's entry as coach in 1959, he took over a losing team and then restoring its glory.

The book also reveals a rather complicated relationship between Lambeau and Lombardi, who were not close. But there was also a mutual respect the two men had for each other and what each had done to earn that respect.

Finally, Names does a great job of detailing the changing NFL. With the emergence of the American Football League, which many thought was just another experiment that would not succeed against the established NFL, Larry shows the early struggles the junior league had and then the gradual acceptance, as the two leagues began battling for draft picks. It eventually led to merger talks by Commissioner Pete Rozelle and others, and finally the merger that would come in 1966.

I've had the pleasure of knowing Larry Names for over 35 years and respect and admire his ability and work, detailing the Packers' history with fascinating stories that allows little Green Bay" claim the title of America's Team."

The book is a winner like the Green Bay Packers have been and still are. I know you'll enjoy The History of the Green Bay Packers: Lombardi's Destiny, Part 3." He was a true winner.

I know I can't wait for Part 4!

Wayne Mausser
Sports Personality and Author

BOOKS IN THE SERIES

LAMBEAU YEARS, THE, PART ONE, THE HISTORY OF THE GREEN BAY PACKERS, VOL. 1

LAMBEAU YEARS, THE, PART TWO, THE HISTORY OF THE GREEN BAY PACKERS, VOL. 2

LAMBEAU YEARS, THE, PART THREE, THE HISTORY OF THE GREEN BAY PACKERS, VOL. 3

SHAMEFUL YEARS THE, THE HISTORY OF THE GREEN BAY PACKERS, VOL. 4

LOMBARDI'S DESTINY, PART ONE, THE HISTORY OF THE GREEN BAY PACKERS, VOL. 5

LOMBARDI'S DESTINY, PART TWO, THE HISTORY OF THE GREEN BAY PACKERS, VOL. 6

LOMBARDI’S DESTINY, PART THREE, THE HISTORY OF THE GREEN BAY PACKERS, VOL. 7

Introduction

One of the bonuses of writing a book such as this one is doing the research it requires. Along that road, the author finds dozens of side stories that don't fit the book but are still quite interesting, often very humorous, and downright informative. You might call them anecdotes or even trivia. Such a tale involves Larry Elkins, the Packers' second 1st Round pick in the 1965 NFL Draft.

After his playing career was cut short by injuries, Elkins worked at jobs that took him to Europe, Africa, and Latin America. In the 1980s, he took up occupations that brought him into close contact with artistic people in the entertainment business. One of those people was Academy Award winner Robert Duvall. Elkins took Duvall all over Texas in search of the perfect accent for his role as Mac Sledge in *Tender Mercies.* When the actor won the statue for his performance, Elkins had a ringside seat at the awards event as Duvall's special guest. When Duvall was cast as Augustus "Gus" McRae in one of my favorite films, *Lonesome Dove*, he called Elkins again to take him around Texas to find the perfect accent for the role. Elkins replied that there would be no need for all that driving because he knew the perfect voice for Duvall. He introduced him to the legendary Sammy Baugh, the former NFL quarterback known as Slingin' Sammy" in his playing days. Duvall studied Baugh for several days in order to get him down." In short, the actor turned the football legend into the legendary screen character Gus McRae.

Being a fan of Duvall and pro football history, the story was truly interesting to me, which is why I shared it here with you.

Another question that I get from my fans and reviewers is, why do I include all the information about the NFL, AFL, AAFC, and other sports teams and leagues in a history of the Green Bay Packers. Well, here's the answer in as few words as possible: I did it for me.

In 1987, I joined Western Writers of America, an organization originally intended to increase the popularity of the only original genre in American literature, the Western novel. I had written four so-called Westerns by then, all published by Doubleday. I made modest sums on each of them but earned no awards or reprints in paperback. Each received fairly good reviews but no movie or television deals. My agent at the time, Ray Puechner (pronounced Peekner), advised me to join WWA to further my career as a novelist. By this time, I had written the first book in the Packers history series, *The History of the Green Bay Packers: The Lambeau Years, Part 1.* Having earned more money off that one book for six weeks of writing and six weeks of sales than I had from the four Westerns combined over eight years, I wasn't sure that Ray's advice that I should join WWA would do me much good. Ray told me I would meet some of the craziest, coolest, and most extraordinary people on this planet at the WWA convention, and I should go. Well, I was wrong, and he was right.

At the first confab I attended in 1987 and held in Sheridan, Wyoming, I did come in contact with those crazy, cool, and extremely extraordinary as well as very talented people on this planet, starting with John Legg, author of some of the greatest mountain man stories you will ever read, with whom I had previously corresponded.

On the first evening there, I happened to make eye-contact with actor David Caruso who was staying at the same hotel where the convention was being held. He wasn't yet the star he would become, but I still thought it was really cool to see a real Hollywood actor in person. Of course, he wasn't the first. Before him, I met *and talked with* the one and only Shirley MacLaine in her dressing room at the Riviera Hotel & Casino in Las Vegas in 1980. What a lady!

Then there was Tom Colgan.

During the first evening at the convention, I saw this young fellow in a denim jacket and blue jeans wandering about the grounds looking lost. My first thought was he was somebody's teenage son trying to look like a cowboy without a hat. Then I heard him speak. Total New York accent. Intrigued, I walked up to him and said, Mets or Yankees?" He said Mets. Then I said, Darn, I thought I was going to like you." He laughed as I explained that I am a Cubs fan. Instantly, we hit it off. We conversed in that universal male language: sports, in this case, Major League Baseball. Not quite like Humphrey Bogart and Claude Rains, but it was the start of a beautiful friendship.

A few days later when our bus broke down on the way back from the Little Bighorn battlefield, another new friend, Frank Roderus, one of the all-time great Western writers, asked me how I came to be so chummy with Tom. I told him exactly what you've already read here, you know, about Tom being some teenage wannabee cowboy. Frank laughed and said, Don't you know who he is?" I replied, Somebody's kid ... another writer here." He laughed and explained that Tom was the Westerns editor for, a major publishing house in New York. Can you believe it? I had my foot in the door with a big-time publisher and didn't even know it at the time. Tom later bought my Slate Creed series, getting me into the big leagues of Westerns. Then he went on to become the editor for several major authors, including Tom Clancy. He's a vice-president at Berkley now.

Ever see the movie *The Hallelujah Trail*? It's one of my favorites of all time because it's absolutely hilarious. Watch it, if you ever get the chance, then tell me I'm not right about it. Like a lot of films, the story is taken from a book. This one was written by Bill Gulick, one of the founders of Western Writers of America. This man was one of my writing heroes, and when I met him, it meant as much to me as meeting Bart Starr, Ray Nitschke, Larry McCarren, James Lofton, Don Beebe, and dozens of others over the past 32 years. But the one Packer I wish I had met, my wife Peg met. He even held her hand.

During his career on the gridiron, players weren't paid all that much, so they had to find jobs to make a living in the off-season. This particular Packer sold class rings to high school students. He came to Peg's high school in Wautoma (WI) when she was a freshman. When he sized the third finger on her right hand, he held her hand, and she was breathless. Why? Because he was the Golden Boy" Heisman Trophy winner from Notre Dame, the one and only Paul Hornung. I imagine how she must have blushed and giggled when he held her hand. Of course, she denies she reacted that way. She was 15 years old, and he was Paul Hornung. And she still thinks I should believe she was calm as a cucumber. Really?

Back to the 1987 WWA convention in Sheridan, Wyoming.

After Bill Gulick, I came into contact with another brilliant writer who also possessed a bit of a twisted sense of humor. His name is Preston Lewis, and he authored this absolutely entertaining series about a guy named Lomax who keeps finding himself searching for that proverbial pot of gold at the end of the rainbow in the Old West but winds up in trouble and a firsthand witness to real history, such as the shootout at the OK Corral.* A single conversation with Preston, where he talked about writing a series of his own, provided the seed for me to create my Slate Creed series.

Then I met the man who gave me the best advice ever shared with me by another author. His name was Dorris Alexander Brown. Don't know that name? How about Dee Brown, the author of the greatest book ever written about the Indigenous People of America, *Bury My Heart at Wounded Knee*? I read it twice, it was that wonderful. Being in total awe of him when I shook his hand and bubbled over him like a schoolgirl meeting Elvis Presley or one of the Beatles, he still let all that go and talked with me about writing. I hung on every word he said in his soft southern drawl. But the most important thing I took from him was simple and to the point. Always remember that you can't take your subject out of the context of history."

Now you know why there's so much information about the NFL, AFL, etc., in these volumes of *The History of the Green Bay Packers: Lombardi's Destiny, Parts 1, 2, 3,* and at least one, and most likely, two more after this one.

Just a little bonus here. Well, more than a little bonus. I don't

**If you like Westerns or the history of the real Old West, I highly recommend you read Preston Lewis's Lomax series. The humor and history in them are simply wonderful. All eight titles can be found on amazon.com/books. I promise, you won't be disappointed.*

read fiction anymore. But I do read lots of non-fiction books. Lately, I've been reading famous film director Frank Capra's autobiography. It's a great book. From his work, I have found a few paragraphs that I would like to share with all Packer fans. Here we go.

Page 78, *Frank Capra: The Name Above the Title*, Capra is writing about his first day at Columbia Pictures.

> *I walked into a hall so narrow even the skinny (people) had to turn sideways to pass. They would have to grease the walls for a pregnant woman. The office cubicles on both sides of the hall were so tiny the entrance doors overlapped.*
>
> *The smell was more concentrated inside—as gamy as the Green Bay Packers' locker room, without windows.* *(My * italics.)*

Page 84, another good quote from Capra's book. He has just left the office of Harry Cohn, president of Columbia.

> *"I left his office feeling I had earned at least a draw with the monster. In the general run of humanity, people either give you a lift, depress you; bore you, or, as with most, leave you indifferent. But not Harry Cohn. Just his presence would make your hackles rise and your adrenals pump furiously. He annoyed and belittled—until he made you hate. Some baseball and football coaches have operated on that principle: John McGraw, Leo Durocher, and Vince Lombardi. Add crudeness and sadism to this principle—and you get Cohn." (Again, my italics.)*

These two paragraphs brought tears of unstoppable laughter when I read them. Although he never said so, I have to believe the great director of *It's A Wonderful Life,* Frank Capra, had to have been a Packer fan.

One last tale from television that proves the Packers are truly America's team.

Remember the TV show *Hill Street Blues*? Look it up, if you don't. I recollect it quite well because of one show where a police officer made a rather ribald remark about a female character named Grace, played by actress Barbara Babcock. He was talking to a patrolman something like this. Word has it she's had relations with the entire Green Bay Packers team." She overheard him and replied —with a giggle, Not the whole team. Just the offensive line." Or words to that affect.

Put that in your pipe and smoke it Brent Musburger, the man who declared the Dallas Cowboys to be America's team. Go back through the years, and you will find more mentions of the Packers in films, radio shows, television shows, and books—non-fiction as well as fiction—than any other professional football team.

§ § §

1

"The Saga of Broadway Joe and the Golden Domer" or When All Hell Broke Loose in Professional Football"

One thing that could always be expected from Vince Lombardi: Never count on him to be predictable.

Using the 1st Round Pick they had obtained in a trade with the Philadelphia Eagles the previous spring, the Green Bay Packers selected Donny Anderson, a halfback from Texas Tech as their number one choice. What was the big deal about this pick? Anderson was only a junior with a year of eligibility remaining in his college career. This made him the first ever junior eligible to be taken in the league's initial round.

When asked why he had chosen Anderson, General Manager Vince Lombardi gave a toothy grin to the reporter who posed the question and said,

Because he was the best player available."

With his next pick, Lombardi laid claim to Larry Elkins, a wide receiver from Baylor. Elkins was also the Number 2 overall pick in the AFL draft, selected by the Houston Oilers. The New York Jets owned the AFL's top pick, originally the property of the Denver Broncos who had received it in a deal with Houston. New York traded the rights to Jerry Rhome, a junior pick from the previous season, to the Oilers. The Jets used the Number 1 choice to draft Joe Namath, quarterback from Alabama who led the Crimson Tide to the NCAA big school national championship. The Jets then used its 2nd Round pick on John Huarte, the Notre Dame quarterback who won the Heisman Trophy after leading the Fighting Irish to a 9-1 record in 1964. Namath was the 1st Round choice of the St. Louis Cardinals, while Huarte was picked in the 6th Round of the NFL draft—76th overall—by the Philadelphia Eagles. This was just the beginning of the saga that could be titled, Joe Willie and the Golden Domer."

Back to the two drafts.

The New York Giants possessed something they hadn't owned since 1951 when they had the bonus pick and took Kyle Rote, the 1950 Heisman Trophy runner-up out of Southern Methodist. This time when the Maras had the first overall pick to make, they chose yet another running back. Immediately, they selected Tucker Frederickson from Auburn. Wellington Mara was sitting outside a Birmingham hotel with a contract in hand and eager to sign the hefty fullback. Tucker penned his name on the deal without hesitation. Terms of the pact were not disclosed by either Mara or Frederickson. Rumors that Tucker planned to sign with Giants were so prevalent on draft day for both leagues that no team in the AFL took a chance on using up a draft choice on him. Score 1 for the NFL.

Although Sonny Werblin and the New York Jets were anxious to get Namath's signature on their contract, nothing could happen with the future Broadway Joe" until he had finished his career with Alabama, which wouldn't be until after the conclusion of the Orange Bowl in Miami on New Year's Day. In the meantime, St. Louis was doing everything it could to persuade Namath to sign with them after the Orange Bowl. No points yet for either league in the Namath chase.

The San Francisco 49ers held the second choice in the NFL draft, and they used it to pick Ken Willard, fullback from North Carolina. Just like Frederickson, Willard went undrafted by the AFL and for the same reason. The 49ers didn't get his John Hancock on a contract nearly as fast as the Giants signed Tucker. However,

Willard did sign his deal a week later. Score another point for the NFL to make the tally: NFL 2, AFL 0.

Joining the Giants in the draft day signing parade were the Los Angeles Rams, Baltimore Colts, and Detroit Lions. LA picked Clarence Clancy" Williams, Jr., an All-American back from Washington State, as their first theft from the AFL. (No, he was not related to Clarence Williams, III, who portrayed Lincoln Hayes in the television series *The Mod Squad.*) The Colts nabbed Mike Curtis, linebacker from Duke, who was chosen by the Kansas City Chiefs in the AFL's 3rd Round. Detroit signed Indiana fullback Tom Nowatzke and Michigan State tackle. The Jets had wanted Nowatzke, while the Boston Patriots had hoped to sign Rush. Add four more points to the NFL side of the ledger. Good start for the older league, but how long would it last?

Monday, the last day of November 1964, brought in several more signed contracts, nearly all by the AFL. The Buffalo Bills led the way with five done deals, including their third pick, Al Atkinson, tackle from Villanova. Previously, the Bills had signed their top choice, tackle Jim Davidson from Ohio State who wasn't drafted by any NFL team. The signing score now stood at: AFL 9, NFL 8.

As for the Packers, Lombardi didn't have to worry about inking Donny Anderson, or any of the other eight futures he selected that year, to deals until the end of the 1965 collegiate playing season. His focus was on Larry Elkins, the other 15 players on this year's list, and the five who were drafted as futures the year before. The current list of eligibles included in drafting order: tackle Alphonse Dotson from Grambling; end 50 from Ole Miss; halfback Wally Mahle from Syracuse; fullback Doug Goodwin from Maryland; tackle Rich Koeper from Oregon State; halfback Bill Symons from Colorado; tackle Roger Jacobazzi from Wisconsin; end Jerry Roberts from Baldwin-Wallace; halfback Junior Coffey from Washington; halfback Larry Bulaich from TCU; halfback Eugene Jeter from Arkansas A&M (now Arkansas-Monticello); fullback John Putnam from Drake; tackle Chuck Hurston from Auburn; kicker Steve Clark from Oregon State; and halfback James Chandler from Benedict College in Columbia, South Carolina.

The futures from 1963 were end Paul Costa from Notre

Dame; tackle Dick Herzing from Drake; back Allen Jacobs from Utah; tackle Alex Zenko from Kent State; back Andrew Ireland from Utah; and linebacker Bill Curry from Georgia Tech.

Besides Anderson as a future, Lombardi named other futures: tackle James Harvey from Ole Miss; end Mike Shinn from Kansas; tackle Rick Marshall from Stephen Austin; tackle Jim Weatherwax from Los Angeles State; guard Roy Schmidt from Long Beach State; fullback Phil Vandersea from UMass; end Jeff White from Texas Tech; and tackle Len Sears from South Carolina.

The first future from the 1964 Draft to sign a pact with the Packers was Bill Curry. End Jerry Roberts from Baldwin-Wallace was the first draftee from the 1965 Draft to put his scrawl on a contract with the Packers. Green Bay lost end Paul Costa from Notre Dame and tackle Chuck Hurston from Auburn to the Buffalo Bills.

Lombardi said the Packers refused to get into a bidding war with the AFL for the services of players.

"We'll make an offer, and that's it."

Lombardi's thinking was influenced by old-timers with the organization. They told how Curly Lambeau nearly bankrupted the club when he tried to outbid the All-America Conference for players right after World War II.

Getting back to the NFL Draft, the Bears had the best hand of any team ever to pick college players because Papa Bear was a wily old fox when it came to finding talent in the bulrushes of collegiate football. He traded with the Pittsburgh Steelers the year before for their 1st Round pick, which turned out to be the number three slot on draft day. Then he owned the 4th pick in the 1st Round by virtue of his Monsters of the Midway playing much less like their nickname in 1964. Wise old owl that he was, he made another trade the year before with Washington for the Redskins 1st Round choice, which turned out to be the 6th pick of the day. With those three 1st Round Picks, Halas chose linebacker Dick Butkus from Illinois, halfback Gayle Sayers from Kansas, and guard Steve DeLong from Tennessee. All three were named to at least five All-American teams. Sayers signed with the Bears, thanks to former NFL great Buddy

Young who urged him to sign with Chicago. Young said,

> ***"Sayers met Mr. (Lamar) Hunt in New York a week ago. The only thing he (Sayers) told me was this. 'When a millionaire opens the door for you, you get a little scared.' My orders were to get Sayers into the National Football League."***

The very personable Young succeeded.

In the meantime, the Packers lost Eugene Jeter to the Denver Broncos, but he wasn't the biggest fish to slip off Lombardi's hook. Larry Elkins, the second 1st Round pick of the Packers, signed with Houston, or should we say, he signed with Houston's millionaire owner Bud Adams.

Lombardi said,

> ***"We made him a reasonable offer." Then he added with a chuckle, We were only outbid by a couple of hundred thousand dollars."***

A Houston newspaper reported Elkins signed for a $35,000 bonus and $100,000 over a three-year period. In addition, Adams was reported to have sweetened the pot even further with the deeds to several pieces of real estate.

> ***"We had no way to compete (with the Oilers), and we wouldn't if we could have," Lombardi said. We have to keep our balance and not go overboard." When asked about the dollar war between the two leagues, Vince said, I don't think it is any war at all. The AFL has a lot of new money from a television contract (with NBC), but they'll find that it doesn't go far."***

Signing Elkins was the fifth No. 1 Pick in six years that the Oilers had corralled. Houston's only failure in the 1st Round was Mike Ditka who signed with Bears in 1961.

About George Halas and his Bears, they split on their other

two 1st Round choices. Dick Butkus, a native of Chicago, the youngest of eight children, and the first to be born in a hospital, announced that he would be signing with the Bears, that he never gave a thought to making a deal with the New York Jets who had obtained the right to him from the Denver Broncos. Sonny Werblin made him a pretty big offer, but Butkus turned down the larger sum to play for the team that had been his favorite while growing up in the Roseland neighborhood on Chicago's south side. A day later Papa Bear lost out on Steve DeLong who signed with the San Diego Chargers.

One of the AFL's prime strategies was to trade the rights to players who wanted to play elsewhere than in the city of the team that drafted them. Dick Butkus not wanting to play in Denver, which was still a mid-size city with a growing metropolitan area in 1965, prompted the Broncos to trade their rights to him to the New York Jets. Executives in the NFL quickly caught on to this tactic.

The Minnesota Vikings knew they had little or no chance to sign end Jack Snow from Notre Dame, so they traded his rights to the Los Angeles Rams for a player to be named later. Being born in Wyoming but raised in California, Snow didn't want to play for a team located in a cold weather city, so he was negotiating with the San Diego Chargers who had made him their 7th Round pick when LA made the deal with the Vikes.

The next Packer draftee to be lost to the AFL was their No. 2 choice Alphonse Dotson who decided to forego his senior year at Grambling for a shot at the pros. A rumor circulated that Dotson had changed his mind and intended to play college ball that autumn, so the Packers backed off from dealing with him. Then the Kansas City Chiefs stepped in and signed him.

The Packers finally signed a draft choice, 6th Round pick safety Bill Symons from Colorado. He was taken by the Chiefs in the 20th Round, but he chose the Packers because they took him earlier in the NFL Draft.

♦♦♦

Sportswriter Bill Halls with *Associated Press* in Detroit reported a major story four days before Christmas 1964.

In an interview with Ralph Wilson, the owner of the Buffalo Bills, Halls learned that an anonymous NFL owner had approached Wilson with a proposal for a merger of the two leagues and a common draft. Wilson, a Detroit insurance and trucking executive and a former stockholder in the NFL's Detroit Lions, also revealed the AFL had received 30 applications for new franchises and hoped to field a team in the Motor City.

> *"About a year ago," said Wilson, one of the top owners in the NFL approached our league with a proposition of merger and a common draft. We called a special meeting to consider it. Our attorneys warned that the Justice Department might jump down our throats on the anti-trust laws. So, we turned it down.*
>
> *"What the NFL wanted (from the AFL) was for us to drop two of our teams. They would take in six, making it a 20-team NFL. One of the teams they wanted us to drop was the New York Jets. It's not likely that the Maras in New York would sit still for a merger with a second team in their city."*

Wilson said he was convinced that major cities, such as New York, Chicago, and Los Angeles could support two teams.

> *"Detroit will definitely have an AFL team. And the move would be more imminent if the city went ahead on plans for a new stadium. But one (a team) is coming within a few years.*
>
> *"Our TV contract was the turning point for our league. There's one thing all this television money will force us to do. We'll*

> *have midweek games, probably sooner than most people believe. I don't object to it. I think it's feasible. If you like football, it doesn't matter whether it's Wednesday night or Sunday."*

Wilson disputed the NFL claim that its football is superior to the AFL brand.

> *"I've always been conservative in my statements, but I have watched the Lions and pro football since 1936, and I "would say the Bills could play with anybody in the NFL. They might win or lose on a given day. That's football. But Buffalo, Boston, San Diego ... they don't have to apologize to anyone, not the Baltimore Colts or the Cleveland Browns. We're their equal and two years from now we'll be stronger than they are. We're signing 40 per cent of the new players and splitting them eight ways, whereas the NFL splits 14 ways. It used to be that, in a given year, an NFL team could come up with two good backs and two good linemen. Now, with the AFL in the picture, they get one of each. It figures we have to be strong. We have been in operation a year longer than the Minnesota Vikings, and they finished third in their NFL race (this year 1964), ahead of the Lions."*

The Bills owner, who still commuted between Buffalo and Detroit to catch Lion home games, said the Bills have signed three of their first four draft choices this year.

> *"We don't feel the NFL beat us in the recent draft. We didn't over-emphasize the draft this*

> ***time. The days of fantastic bonuses given to college prospects are gone."***

Apparently, Wilson was unaware of the deal Bud Adams of the Houston Oilers had given Larry Elkins. Nor was he in contact with Sonny Werblin about his thoughts and intentions on the draft. His knowledge of the history of the AFL was a little lacking as well.

> ***"When we formed the league eight (his error, not mine) years ago without players or stadiums, we paid top dollar for everybody we got. Why pay it now? Why give great bonuses to kids who might not make your ball club? There's the difference. Now we have the players."***

Wilson admitted that the AFL had sent proposals to the NFL for a championship game between the AFL title winner and the NFL champion.

> ***"We'd like a playoff, and one should be held. But we're not going to them again with our hat in our hand. There won't be a title playoff between the two leagues unless some third party arranges it."***

A third party? Meaning what? A television network with a load of cash in hand?

The answer was not as far away as many of the owners, league commissioners, pro football fans, *and* television moguls were thinking back then. But sportswriters? Sportswriters have always speculated about the future. If they don't, they're soon peddling newspapers instead of writing for them.

Jack Cuddy, sportswriter for *United Press International* in New York, had this to offer after the two leagues played their respective title games just before the New Year.

> ***"Two professional football classics over the weekend at Buffalo and Cleveland were***

> *powerful indicators that an annual championship game between the NFL and AFL winners must become a reality soon because of the tremendous live-spectator and home-TV interest in the sport. Neither the NFL nor the AFL title games, nor a potential title game will ever be shifted to southern cities merely because of northern cold weather.*
>
> *The two title games played over the weekend drew capacity crowds: 40,242 in Buffalo and 79,544 in Cleveland. No one was frozen at either game because the weather had turned mild for those locations. However, the tickets were sold in very cold weather preceding the holiday period. The heavy advance sales proved that torrid gridiron fans would mush to the Arctic, perhaps, to watch their heroes score touchdowns and kick field goals.*
>
> *In this connection, it should be emphasized that the three most recent NFL title games were played in Chicago, New York, and Green Bay, Wisconsin."*

A representative of the Cleveland Browns boasted,

> *"We could have sold 130,000 to 150,000 tickets to Sunday's game, regardless of the weather. Remember, our attendance this year for our eight home games at Municipal Stadium averaged 79,000."*

Another indicator of the tremendous interest in the pro game was the fact that it was then commanding millions of dollars from

TV and radio broadcasting. The Cleveland game received approximately $1,800,000 from those sources. For 1964, this was a huge payday.

For 1965, the AFL would be starting its new five-year deal with the National Broadcasting Company that would pay the circuit a cool $34 million. And should the league expand during that period, each new franchise would benefit for the tidy sum—back then—of $500,000.

That AFL-NBC contract had done much to end any wild talk about the NFL absorbing some of the AFL clubs in a merger like the senior circuit did in 1950 with the All-America Football Conference. More so, the pact could be a lever in boosting demand for a title game between the two leagues.

♦♦♦

Chapter 2 of the saga Broadway Joe and the Golden Domer" hit the sports pages on December 30 when *Associated Press* writer Mike Rathet scooped the story that Joe Namath had been offered $100,000 a year for three years and $89,000 in a bonus that included a new limousine. That would make Namath, the son of a Beaver Falls, Pennsylvania gas station attendant, the highest priced rookie of all time—at least until then. So said Rathet who was in Miami to cover the Orange Bowl. He claimed to have wheedled the news out of sources close to Namath and the Jets."

"It's more than that,"

said a spokesman for the St. Louis Cards who were in Miami to play the Packers in the Playoff Bowl. Of course, the blabbermouth from River City wished to remain anonymous.

At the same time, another passing whiz, Tulsa's Jerry Rhome, penned his name to a deal with the Dallas Cowboys. He went with the NFL team, although he was offered bales of greenbacks by the AFL's Houston Oilers owner Bud Adams.

Just for fun, Georgia's All-America tackle Jim Wilson allegedly signed two contracts—one in each league. The two teams in question were the Boston Patriots and the San Francisco 49ers. Wilson's deal with Boston was allegedly signed in August before the Pats even drafted him. The 49ers signed Wilson after he played his last collegiate game, the Sun Bowl on December 26. Of course, legal wrangling would ensue, but it led to nothing. Frisco landed Wilson for one season. Even though he made the All-Rookie Team, the 49ers put him on the expansion pool and he was chosen by the fledgling Atlanta Falcons, where he lasted two seasons before being traded to the Los Angeles Rams as part of a two-for-one deal. He tore up a knee in camp before the 1969 campaign then hurt his back in the first pre-season game the following year. Surgery on the knee and his back ended his career.

There was one other big name signing on December 29, and wouldn't you just know it? George Halas pulled another rabbit out of his hat. This time he landed the man who was the top rusher and top scorer in college football for 1964. The really weird part about it all was this guy wasn't even drafted by either league. Now how does that figure? Oh, yes, the player. His name was Brian Piccolo, a fullback out of Wake Forest.

So, why wasn't Piccolo drafted? Wake Forest was a member of the Atlantic Coast Conference, which was one of the worst leagues in the country that year. Not one of their eight schools finished with a winning record. In their non-conference games, the league won 10, lost 17, and tied one. Of those 10 wins, seven were over second level teams. In short, the ACC of 1964 was not on par with the SEC, Big 10, Big 12, Pacific Coast Conference, and Notre Dame. Therefore, nearly every pro scout considered Piccolo's statistics to be tarnished by the fact he played against such inferior competition. Everyone except Papa Bear Halas. Piccolo was so overlooked and disrespected that he didn't even get selected for the College All-Star team.

The Dallas office of *United Press International* released a really provocative story in the sports pages across the country on the second day of the New Year. Basically, the article concerned the early signings of some players, primarily with AFL teams. The unknown writer of the piece wrote that one of the guilty parties was

> ***"Minnesota of the AFL."*** ***(Probably a typo committed by the typesetter.)***

He seemed to know more about the college game than the

pros. The theme of the story supported the colleges losing players just before bowl games because these lunkheads signed contracts with pro teams. These early signings did one good thing for the pro game. They gave the NCAA some ammunition that allowed the colleges to join the cold war between the NFL and AFL. Threatened legal action as well as seeking help from the federal government—never a very good thing—to protect their interests—meaning having all those young athletes toiling away for them for as long as they could without giving them any monetary compensation other than a free education and four years of free room and board—really made the commissioners of the NFL and AFL sit up and pay closer attention to the meandering checkbooks of the teams under their auspices. The battles between the leagues were expanding exponentially, and sooner or later one—or both—of the leagues just might have to pay a very heavy price for their questionable actions.

♦♦♦

This brings us to the next episode of the theme for this chapter, *The Saga of Broadway Joe and the Golden Domer" or When All Hell Broke Loose within Professional Football.*

The Alabama Crimson Tide played the Texas Longhorns in the Cotton Bowl on January 1. Joe Namath played the whole game on a knee that he had injured in practice on the previous Monday, four days earlier. Courageous as he was, Namath couldn't pull off a victory in the fourth quarter. On the next day, he made history that changed the world of sports forever.

Ben Funk of *Associated Press* called it,

> ***"The Horatio Alger story of the former shoeshine boy who led Alabama to the national college championship ... climaxed at a luxury hotel at Miami Beach.***
>
> ***Where he concluded a deal with the New York Jets of the (AFL) that ... will bring him $400,000 for three years work."***

Sonny Werblin, president of the Jets, said,

> *"I'm sure it pays the largest amount ever given to a young athlete in any sport." He added, ... the cat-quick Namath was a bargain at the price. We feel that in getting Joe, we got the No. 1 college football player in America, and with him we will give New York fans the finest team in America. This is the start toward many championship years for the Jets."*

Werblin's remarks may have been a wishing-well full of pipe dreams, but one thing for certain was the signing of "Broadway Joe" rocked the world and turned the NFL owners into catatonic zombies for the near future. All the senior circuit moguls could do was wait to see what the other owners in the junior loop would do. After all, Namath wasn't the only superstar still unsigned.

Namath had a few choice words to say about his deal that gave his plethora of new fans a taste of his lovable, outlandish, even boyish assessments on just about any topic of the moment. He revealed how the St. Louis Cardinals kept bidding right along with the Jets until the New York offer reached four hundred grand. That was more than the Redbirds could handle.

> *"I took both teams into consideration. I wanted more money." Wearing a pink sportscoat, he grinned, showing off his pearly whites and his twinkling blue eyes. I was interested in the coach and the organization. New York City is a fine place. The sports fans are great, and Weeb Ewbank is an outstanding coach."*

Cleveland quarterback Frank Ryan stated bluntly that if Namath was

> *"worth $400,000, I'm worth a million."*

You can bet that sent a real shiver down the spines of owners in both leagues.

As for Namath, now the world was *his* oyster.

♦♦♦

A little aside here to show a sign of the times.

At their annual meeting right after the New Year, the NFL Players Association came up with one of the goofiest ideas ever. They announced that they planned to present the club owners with a plan to play a best-of-three series instead of a single championship game. Game one would be played in one division winner's stadium, and game two would be played in the other division champion's playground. The third game, if necessary, would be played in a neutral city.

Why would they propose such an idiotic plan? They wanted more money to go into the players' pension fund as well as in the pockets of the players in the extra game or two. Who can blame them for that? At the moment, the fund was getting squat added each year. They deserved a better plan. But there had to be a better way to get it.

Those representatives from each team's players evidently had taken too many hits to their helmets. A best-of-three series? Someone needed to tell them they played football, not baseball, not basketball, not even hockey or badminton. They should have known more than anyone that football is not a contact sport. It's a collision sport, much like a demolition derby. Basketball is a contact sport. Hockey is also a collision sport, but it involves fewer players chasing a little rubber disk with sticks in their gloved hands who only slam into an opponent once before a fist fight breaks out. Pro football at this time involved two teams lining up across from each other and then throwing themselves violently at each other an average of 120 times a game. It's hard to imagine two teams wanting to do that two Sundays in a row to each other. The loser of the first game would surely play harder and meaner in the second game, while the winner of the first game would retaliate in brawl number two whenever there was the slightest insult— physically or verbally—hurled at them.

Football is a gladiatorial competition, only without the

swords and tridents, and not as much blood. Two teams going at each other three Sundays straight could literally end up in a last-man-standing affair. Just imagine the Bears and Packers squaring off three weeks in succession. Sends chills down the spine to think of how many good players might wind up with career-ending injuries. The same would happen in a clash between division champs going toe-to-toe three weeks in a row.

Let me repeat. This was one of the goofiest and dumbest ideas ever put forward by men who played the game. Blame their nitwit idea on too many blocks and tackles since childhood in a time where no one had yet figured out the need for concussion protocol.

♦♦♦

Associated Press sportswriter Murray Chass reported another salvo of complaints fired by the NCAA at the two pro football leagues. As they had been doing for the past five years, their aim was to get the two circuits to play nice together … or else.

The two leagues were once again headed for court battles with each other. What was the argument this time? Who owned the rights to the services of four Oklahoma players who signed with teams in each league *before their college eligibility expired.* The question was simple. Were their early signings by Minnesota and Houston legal or null and void?

A bigger problem confronting the two belligerent leagues was whether they planned to co-operate with the colleges and each other in eliminating the practices that had aroused the wrath of college officials. Or would the pros continue to ignore each other *and* the righteous indignation of the collegiate representatives?

Executive Director Walter Byers of the National Collegiate Athletic Association (NCAA) was hopeful but also realistic about the prospects of cooperation among the three potential combatants.

> ***"We have urged these people to set their drafts back until after January 1, but they have refused to do it. We've met with them before but not with both leagues together."***

Byers wanted a joint meeting with representatives from both

leagues. If not, then the NCAA hinted that legal action might be the next step to take. Of course, the owners in both loops didn't want that because lawyers don't come cheap. Paying attorneys to defend them for their bull-headed attitudes cost bales of greenbacks.

The AFL's second in command Milt Woodard, stated openly that his league would be glad to meet with the NCAA officials and work out a plan that would satisfy both parties, meaning the colleges and the two pro circuits. However, this would never happen unless the NFL also agreed to the meeting. For the time being, Pete Rozelle had no comment on the matter, which, in matters like this one, he had to get the advice of several owners before taking such a step. For the present, the status between the leagues and the NCAA would sadly remain the same. Heaven forbid that anyone should tamper with the status quo.

♦♦♦

Long time Packer standout Dave Hawg" Hanner made his say-so for the press about the big bonuses the 1965 crop of rookies were getting from the junior circuit.

> *"A man who gets that much money usually doesn't want to pay the price" to become an outstanding professional football player. If he doesn't like it (pro football), what with a no-cut contract, he can quit as soon as his contract runs out."*

Of course, Hanner was referring mostly to Joe Namath and his $400,000 deal.

> *"I saw Namath play in the Orange Bowl against Texas. He looked great, but he will have to make a big improvement to look that good in the pros. You can't blame the boys for taking the money, but when you pay that much for a player, you have to play him, and if he doesn't do well, then you're going to have dissension on the ball club and friction is the worst thing you can have on a club."*

The 13-year pro was right—for the moment. Only time would tell whether Namath and the other bonus babies would earn their huge paydays.

♦♦♦

The final chapter of The Saga of Broadway Joe and the Golden Domer" was yet to be written, although some assumed it had when John Huarte scratched his signature on a pro contract. If he had signed with the Philadelphia Eagles, the NFL club that drafted the winner of the 1964 Heisman Trophy, then no tale connecting the two quarterbacks would have been told. Instead, Huarte inked a pact with—wait for it—the same New York team as Namath had. If the Jets had gotten the Notre Dame standout for the usual signing bonus, nobody would have made a big deal of the agreement, except for one little item. The amount of Huarte's pact amounted to exactly half of Namath's deal. The Golden Domer's contract called for several items that added up to $200,000.

So why would Sonny Werblin pay so much for two men who played the same position? Insurance! Namath had a gimpy knee that would be operated on that spring. There was no telling when he would be back to full speed, if ever. Huarte's body was perfectly healthy and suitable for the normal wear and tear of professional football. Thus, he was the insurance policy for Namath. Smart move by Werblin, even if it did cost the Jets another two hundred grand.

The next chapter of The Saga of Broadway Joe and the Golden Domer" wouldn't come until training camp that summer when the two quarterbacks squared off for the starting position.

§ § §

2

The Cold War Continues

The AFL All-Star game was scheduled to be held Saturday, January 16, in New Orleans. A bad case of Old South inhospitality forced it to be canceled and moved to Houston. Racial discrimination raised its ugly head at a time when it should have been buried once and for all time on Juneteenth 1865. A hundred years later it was still alive and as putrid as it had ever been throughout the South and much of the industrial North. Sadder yet, racism continues to live to this day in pockets of our nation. Only now, it's not as open as it was in 1965 in Louisiana. Even worse, today's victims have become far more openly bitter toward those who disdain minorities than did their ancestors causing a social schism that may go on and on for who knows how long.

Before the All-Star game and the AFL league meeting were canceled, 21 players of color who were to play in the game packed their bags and left the city.

> ***"We're not wanted here, so we are leaving," said halfback Clem Daniels of the Oakland Raiders. We all encountered similar problems Saturday night. We were refused cab service and admittance to French Quarter clubs. We came here to relax and enjoy ourselves and put on a great game. You can't do those things under existing circumstances."***

AFL Commissioner Joe Foss said,

> ***"Since all players are part of the official league family, the league must abide by their decision not to play."***

Foss chose the right path in following the lead of the players. David Dixon headed the group sponsoring the All-Star game with the hopes it would lead the AFL owners to grant his group a franchise in the junior circuit. He worked frantically to get the players to change their minds by arranging for them to have access to all the better class establishments in the French Quarter. His efforts went for naught as the players decided to leave together because the treatment that they were receiving began with the taxi service at the airport when they tried to hire cabs to take them to their hotels.

Before making their final decision to pull out of the game, Dixon told reporters,

> ***"If they walk out, this blows pro football for New Orleans."***

He and his group had been trying for four years to gain a franchise for New Orleans in either league. Dixon was right as far as the AFL was concerned, but the owners in the NFL had other ideas. Apparently, Washington Redskins owner George Marshall wasn't the only racist mogul in the senior circuit.

Bill Sullivan, president of the Boston Patriots, said he was truly sorry for Dixon because the discrimination incidents involving the AFL players:

> ***"just about wrecks all his hopes for an AFL franchise."***

New Orleans Mayor Victor Schiro* said the players had:

> ***"done themselves and their race a disservice, not to mention the almost irreparable harm they inflicted on the future of professional football in New Orleans."***

Translation: Schiro was saying it was acceptable for the Caucasian

**Victor Schiro just happened to be the name of my one-time golf partner. He and the mayor of New Orleans were not related. I tell you this because I modeled at least one character in each of my novels after my late friend. I did that because he was a man of real class and a fine friend. He made me a better golfer and also a better person. Vic loved the Packers.*

businessmen and taxi drivers to be racist, while the players should have accepted their places in the so-called social order long in practice in The Big Easy."

Joe Foss failed to address the racism issue with his comments, but had he done so, he would have fanned the flames of racism in the South.

> ***"Expansion is nothing immediate and is some time away as yet. Let the future take care of the situation so far as New Orleans is concerned. It is just a case of time."***

Foss always was good at dodging bullets; his war record was proof of that. But he was right about the racial situation in the South. It was just a case of time and some long-awaited amendments toe U.S. Constitution to bring a semblance of racial equality to America.

Some players of color were admitted to two French Quarter nightspots, both owned by musicians. Al Hirt's Bourbon Street Club welcomed the players and even introduced them to the audience who responded with a rousing ovation. Pete Fountain's establishment was also hospitable to the players. Hirt and Fountain planted the seeds of integration that would take years to bear real fruit in NOLA. But only a pair of night spots treating them with dignity was not enough for the players of color. They still voted the next day to walk out. Who could blame them?

The final two straws to land on this camel's back came from a local television station and from the sports editor of a newspaper.

WDSU-TV, one of the South's major television stations, asked editorially,

> ***"Was it fair for the players to unleash unfavorable publicity on the entire city and***

> ***state for the actions of a few cab drivers and Bourbon Street night club operators? We believe the players, in walking out, lost sight of the fact that a great many civic leaders worked hard and long to see that the athletes had a pleasant, comfortable stay in the city."***

Translation: What's the big deal? Nobody threatened to lynch any of them. So why the walkout?

Bill McIntyre of the *Shreveport Times* wrote in his column that the decision to pull out of New Orleans indicates the AFL is still in its infancy" and undeserving of a playoff with the NFL.

> ***"The AFL chose to take dictation from a minority group, and we couldn't care less whether they were Negroes, Caucasians, or monsters, which provides evidence they have forfeited all pretense of public trust and support."***

Translation: Bow down, boys, and mind your place among decent folks.

The position taken by the television station and the sports editor could only be described with one word: RACIST. Both refused to accept those immortal words of Bob Dylan, the poet laureate of that decade and many years after, who wrote and sang so eloquently, The times they are a-changing," and the answer is blowin' in the wind." None of those racist fools could stop it. Not just for people of one color but for people of every color all around the world. Humanity was pulling the toes of one foot out of the muck of bigotry and beginning the march toward racial equality for everyone. Now more than a half century later humanity is still working on getting its whole foot out of the slime of bias and intolerance. How much longer will it take for humanity to rise above the stench of our ancestors?

♦♦♦

For years, the NFL teams had used assistant college coaches and former NFL players as part-time talent scouts. The AFL followed this practice as well when it joined the pro ranks in 1960. Nobody in the college ranks seemed to mind until the pros began signing players before their college eligibility had expired.

When the NCAA officials began looking at ways to stop the pro leagues from this unethical system of acquiring talent, they hit upon the idea of punishing the pros by forbidding assistant coaches from scouting for them. How to do that? Punish the colleges where these assistants worked. This system worked when the only major pro league was the NFL, but it always broke down when the senior loop had competition, starting back in 1926 when the first AFL came into temporary existence with Red Grange as its showcase star.

Again, the NCAA asked the two pro leagues to delay their drafts until after the New Year's Day bowl games. Each league said they would do that if the other league complied as well. The problem with that was neither league trusted the other to keep its word to the NCAA. Thus, another system had to be arranged and made acceptable to all three parties. Of course, that proposal was a mutual draft by the two pro leagues. That wasn't going to happen until the two leagues merged, and a merger was simply out of the question for the moment.

♦♦♦

The National Broadcasting Company upped the ante for the AFL with a deal that would give the network the rights to the junior league's championship game and All-Star game for the next five years. NBC coughed up another $7,000,000 for those rights to go along with the $36,000,000 for the rights to the regular season games over that same time period. Both the broadcaster and the league were anticipating the circuit would expand by two more franchises in that time period, so allowances were made for that possibility as well.

This deal assured the AFL and its fans that their teams stood on solid financial ground, especially since the Big Apple Jets now had Broadway Joe Namath and Golden Domer Johnny Huarte under contract for three year of the five years of their TV contract.

♦♦♦

Darrell Royal, coach of the Texas Longhorns, lost any love he might have had for the AFL because the New York Jets were interested in signing George Sauer, Jr., Royal's prize receiver. Sauer still had another year of eligibility left in his college career because he had been redshirted as a sophomore. He had some assistance with his decision to go pro early. His father was the Jets' director of personnel.

Royal was incensed that Sauer would leave his team.

> ***"We've wet-nursed him through three years and toughened him up, and now, just when we're ready to capitalize on him, bam, he's gone."***

The Texas coach threatened to ban all AFL personnel from the university if the Jets signed Sauer.

> ***"I hate to get into a hassle over this, but a man has to stand up for what is right."***

Sauer was not the only redshirt leaving his college team. Eight other players who had been redshirted as underclassmen had already signed with teams in both leagues, four to each circuit.

At the same time, the Southeastern Conference voted to deny any and all AFL personnel from their athletic facilities. Their reason for this action was the AFL's refusal to stop signing players who still had eligibility remaining in their college careers.

Legally, the AFL had every right to sign these redshirts because their original class was graduating in June. The SEC athletic directors weren't concerned with legalities. Their only consideration was for the success of their football teams' win-and-loss records and how many fans they would squeeze into their stadiums. As usual, money was the bottom line instead of the welfare of the student-athlete.

AFL Commissioner Joe Foss attacked redshirting as a selfish practice that only benefited the colleges. He pointed out that several other colleges didn't redshirt their student-athletes. Many of these opponents of the system were private schools, such as Notre Dame, Rice, and Northwestern. He made a good point with this remark, one that still hasn't been addressed properly in the college ranks.

In early February, Foss announced that the AFL had agreed not to sign any college players until after their school had completed its season, including bowl game appearances. Players could still be drafted but not signed. Foss also stated that the AFL would continue to hold its draft on the weekend after Thanksgiving Day.

A week later the NFL moguls met in Palm Desert, California, a community 14 miles east of the more well-known city of the stars, Palm Springs. Their first order of business was to set the calendar for the coming season. They voted to start the 1965 campaign a week later than usual in order to avoid the usual hassle of competing with Major League Baseball for fans and the use of stadiums that were primarily used for the summer game, such as Wrigley Field in Chicago and Metropolitan Stadium in Minneapolis. Next, they agreed to play the league title game on January 2, 1966, allowing a week off for the two division winners or for playoff games in either or both divisions. Then they held a vote on whether they should work out some sort of deal with the AFL on refraining from signing draftees before they finished their playing seasons. That vote went 12 in favor and two opposed, the two naysayers being the San Francisco 49ers and New York Giants, the only clubs in direct competition with AFL teams, the New York Jets and Oakland Raiders. The owners agreed to follow the example of their AFL counterparts and allow the commissioner to set fines or other penalties for any future violations, such as Minnesota's signing three Oklahoma players before their bowl game and making them ineligible to play.

This was a major step by the NFL owners toward the eventual goal of a common draft, a championship game between the two league winners, and interleague exhibition games. Leading the charge to that end was none other Papa Bear himself, George Stanley Halas, Sr. He let it be known to the media that the day for this to happen would be in the near future. Only one obstacle stood in the way: a change to the NFL's constitution which had to be approved by all 14 franchises. This was not likely to happen because the owners were notorious for hardly ever voting unanimously on anything except the league's exhibition season schedule.

The owners renewed the roster limit to 40 players, but in a new wrinkle, they finally acknowledged the existence of the taxi squad. They hated the name, but no one could come up with a better one.

Another rare hint—that the NFL was admitting the rival league existed—came when the owners approved a promotional deal with soft drink manufacturer Coca-Cola. The year before Coca-Cola started a program where they would put pictures of NFL players under their bottle caps. For 1965, Coke wanted to mix their NFL bottle caps with their AFL bottle caps. When customers collected an entire team, they were given prizes. The NFL owners agreed to this.

Pete Rozelle called this promotion a great thing for his league, then added with a grin,

> ***"This is in no way connected with a common draft between the two leagues."***

Pete simply could not keep a straight face when fiddling with the truth.

Oddly, the NFL owners refused to discuss a common draft and a championship game with the AFL when asked to do so by their commissioner. They adjourned, packed their bags, and went home until their next meeting in the spring.

♦♦♦

After four months of haggling with the NCAA the pro leagues agreed to stop signing college players before their final college game, meaning bowl games but not all-star games. The rules adopted by the NFL were quickly adopted by the AFL. Peace between the pros and colleges was still not achieved, but this truce worked for the time being.

♦♦♦

While the NFL and AFL were still fighting over signing college players before their eligibility was completed, a new kid came walking along the pro football block. The Continental Football League was created out of the remnants of the defunct United Football League and the still active Atlantic Coast Football League, both of them minor leagues located primarily in the East.

The COFL (the O" placed in the initials of the league to distinguish it from the CFL, the Canadian Football League) planned to begin play in the fall of 1965 with 10 teams divided into two divisions. Philadelphia would be the only major U.S. city to have a team in the fledgling circuit. Newark, New Jersey would represent the New York metropolitan area. Toronto was considered to be major city, although located in Canada. Charleston and Wheeling, West Virginia and Fort Wayne, Indiana were also absorbed from the UFL. Hartford, Connecticut; Springfield, Massachusetts; and Richmond, Virginia left the ACFL to join the new loop. Newark also departed the ACFL with the hopes of being a successful competitor with the New York Giants and New York Jets. The owners planned to put a team in Providence, Rhode Island, which would give the COFL 10 teams.

"This will not be a minor league,"
said Alex Schoenbaum, one of the owners of the Charleston team.

> ***"This will be a major league. Ours will be a league stretching from Canada to the Gulf of Mexico. We are throwing away salary restrictions and plan to go big time all the way. We are dealing with men able to finance big budgets, such as those in the National and American Leagues. We'll bid for top player talent. We'll go for big crowds and national television."***

At the time, early February, the COFL was hoping to place franchises in Miami and New Orleans. By the end of the month, the new league had applications from promoters in 11 different cities across the nation: Washington, Chicago, Las Vegas, Cincinnati, Miami, New Orleans, New York, Norfolk (Virginia), Oklahoma City, Omaha, and Charlotte (North Carolina).

By the middle of March, the owners of the Springfield Acorns announced that their negotiations to sell their franchise in the COFL had collapsed and that they were considering moving their team to another city. To where they were thinking of moving was not yet known.

A week later the COFL hired former Major League Baseball commissioner A.B. Happy" Chandler to be the first commissioner of the new circuit. The owners gave Chandler a five-year contract worth $50,000 per year. Chandler approached the Columbia Broadcasting System with a plan for the network to telecast the new league's playoff games. He suggested a 13-week round robin playoff to be held January through March. CBS found the idea interesting because football was big on TV already—and growing bigger every season—and those three months had no games for the present. A single sponsor had been lined up by mid-May, but CBS had not yet committed to any deal.

As far as the NFL and AFL were concerned, the new circuit posed no threat to either of them. The NFL still had a contract with CBS, and the AFL was just beginning their new pact with NBC that would run through 1969. This only left ABC as a possible venue for the COFL, but the brass at that network had no interest in the new loop because they had not done well with the AFL.

Chandler predicted the COFL would be a major league in four or five years. All the circuit needed to reach that status was a television contract. That hardly seemed likely in 1965 when nearly all the sports news buzzed around the possibility of the NFL and AFL merging.

♦♦♦

Getting down to the nitty-gritty of a possible merger between the NFL and AFL, a *Sports Illustrated* article stated that one day soon the two established leagues would have to come together as one league, or both might go broke if they didn't. And the survivor would be … the COFL … by default? At this point in professional football history, it could have happened. No, really, it could have happened. Think about it. History could repeat itself. All the two leagues had to do was continue to gamble on signing the best rookie players for huge bonuses. Point of fact, the acquisitions of Joe Namath and John Huarte. More than half the teams in both leagues didn't have the money to equal the deal the Domer received and none of them had the bucks to match the deal Broadway Joe was handed.

But let's not get ahead of ourselves here. Back to the article in *Sports Illustrated.*

The magazine's writer broke down the new league that would

be created by a merger and a two-team expansion. The new entity would consist of two coast-to-coast conferences, each retaining their designations as National and American. Then the conferences would be divided into two divisions, one Eastern and one Western as follows:

National Conference, ***Eastern Division:*** Colts, Redskins, Eagles, Giants, Patriots, and Bills;
Western Division: Packers, Bears, Cowboys, Chargers, Oilers, and Raiders.

American Conference, ***Eastern Division:*** Browns, Lions, Steelers, Jets, Atlanta, and New Orleans;
Western Division: Cardinals, Vikings, Rams, 49ers, Chiefs, and Broncos.

Of course, Atlanta and New Orleans would be the most logical expansion teams. Also, each division would have six teams, making scheduling rather interesting. Both leagues had been playing 14-game regular seasons, meaning seven at home and seven on the road. In the NFL, each team played the other six teams in their division home and away, and then they played two games against teams in the other bunch. In the AFL, each team played every other team twice, no matter the divisions. Could the NFL return to its pre-expansion schedule of 12 games? Not after playing two years of having 14 per season. Same with the AFL franchises. So, how would the two circuits deal with the four non-division contests? A moot question until a merger emerged from a secret confab of the owners at some point in the future.

This particular plan purported by the magazine existed in more than one pro executive's mind, and no one connected with the sport was willing to bet against something like this happening and happening very soon.

The *Sports Illustrated* writer concluded his piece with his final prognostication.

> ***"Everybody knows that pro football is going to achieve that peace someday. Bonuses to rookie players cannot keep on going up. And the general public continues to move closer,***

emotionally, to the day when it will either get a true title game between the two leagues or drag NFL Commissioner Pete Rozelle through the streets.

The most logical thing to expect, certainly within two years and perhaps as early as next December, is a reorganization along these lines: A common draft, a playoff game, one commissioner, and two league presidents, both leagues keeping their identity and current opponents, except that the AFL would expand to 10 clubs, taking in Atlanta and New Orleans or Philadelphia."

The guy who wrote this article just might have been the reincarnated spirit of Nostradamus, the great French prophet of the 16th Century. Or maybe he was just smart enough to put two and two together and actually come up with four.

One might ask why he put Philadelphia into the mix of getting an expansion team in the AFL. Go back three pages to find the answer. Or read the book, *Halas on Halas*, to find the story about how and why the New York Giants came into the NFL. Lot of fiction in Papa Bear's personal tome, but this particular anecdote carries more than a grain of truth to it.

♦♦♦

After four months of negotiations with the NCAA, the NFL and AFL agreed to stop the premature signing of college players. In addition, the two pro leagues invoked stiff penalties for violators. This accord was a huge step in the direction of a merger between the senior league and the upstart AFL.

The NFL and its junior partner stated they wouldn't sign any player until his team had completed its varsity season, including bowl games. Then, and only then, the pro aggregates could continue their bidding war for new talent. The NFL had already adopted rules calling for tough penalties for infractions, including the possible loss by a club of all its draft choices. Then the AFL agreed to implement the same regulations.

At the same time, the NCAA approved a regulation prohibiting college coaches, assistant coaches, and trainers from moonlighting as scouts for the pro teams. Staff members of NCAA institutions were still permitted to give out information about student athletes, but they were denied any direct or indirect compensation from the pro teams. This was another step in the direction of a merger between the two pro leagues.

♦♦♦

On Thursday June third, Commissioner Pete Rozelle announced he had recommended to the NFL owners that they add two more teams to their league by 1967.

Informed of Rozelle's idea, Commissioner Joe Foss of the rival AFL said his league might do the same and possibly sooner, perhaps putting two new teams on the field by 1966.

Rozelle revealed a list of cities with applicants for franchises. The list consisted of Montreal, Toronto, Boston, Miami Atlanta, New Orleans, Cincinnati, Houston Memphis, Phoenix, Seattle, and Portland. Of the two Canadian cities, the commissioner expressed his concerns about disrupting the Canadian Football League. He explained that it would be unwise to do anything detrimental to the CFL. When one reporter pointed out that Boston and Houston already had teams in the AFL, Rozelle said he hadn't thought much about those cities in particular.

Foss had other ideas. He said there was plenty of room for both leagues to expand and several that could support two teams. He listed Chicago, Washington DC, Philadelphia, Los Angeles, Milwaukee, Atlanta, New Orleans, Miami, Portland, Louisville, Memphis, Seattle, Montreal, Toronto, Vancouver, Columbus and Dayton, Ohio. Foss added that the most likely pair to join the AFL would be Philadelphia and Atlanta when the owners were scheduled to meet in the following week.

The Philly applicants for an AFL franchise were a group of investors headed by former West Point Coach Earl Red" Blaik and Joseph McCrane, GM of Garden State Park racetrack. McCrane, son-in-law of Eugene Mori operating head of both Hialeah and Garden

State tracks, played under Blaik at West Point, which led to their association in the AFL venture. Their plan was to make Blaik the GM of the new franchise and hire Vince Lombardi away from the Packers. These people were dead serious about breaking into the junior circuit.

Recognizing the gravity of the AFL's determination to expand the league in 1966, the NFL owners directed Rozelle to hire a private market research organization to investigate the potential of prospective new league cities. Pete said he expected to have the name of at least one city or possibly two by the following winter meeting in February. He added that expansion could most likely bring realignment of the present NFL conference structure, possibly splitting each conference into two four-team divisions.

All of this expansion talk by both leagues had been precipitated by the failure of the two leagues to come to an agreement on a mutual college draft. A common draft was considered by outsiders to be the initial step in reaching a merger of the two leagues.

Upon hearing Rozelle's views at his press conference on June 3, several reporters speculated on how the NFL would be realigned for the future. First, they opined the two expansion franchises would be in Atlanta and Houston. Both teams would be added to the Eastern Conference and the St. Louis Cardinals would be shifted out West. Then the Eastern Conference would be divided into Northern and Southern Divisions. The North would consist of Cleveland, New York, Philadelphia, and Washington, and the South would be Atlanta, Baltimore, Dallas, and Houston. The Western eight would be split into the Midwest Division and Western Division. Chicago, Detroit, Green Bay, and Pittsburgh would land in the Midwest, and the West would consist of Los Angeles, Minnesota, St. Louis, and San Francisco.

Next these giants of the press speculated on the expansion of the AFL in 1966. The Houston Oilers would be moved into the West Division, while the East would absorb the two new franchises, which would be Atlanta and Philadelphia. Atlanta because it would keep the NFL out of the southeast, and the City of Brotherly Love because the best coach in pro football would be snatched away from the haughty senior league. Of course, that man was Vincent Lombardi.

Also, behind the move to place an AFL franchise in Philly was the NBC television network. The television moguls knew all too well that professional football ratings were on a rapid rise, meaning bigger bucks from advertisers of Sunday programming, and of course, that would be pro football.

The AFL had already scheduled a meeting of owners in New Jersey for the following Monday and Tuesday. Their single purpose was expansion for the next year. They intended to accept a pair of applicants to join them. Foss said that to say that they would be Atlanta and Philadelphia was guesswork because the owners had 50 or more applications.

Further supposition by the reporters focused on Atlanta being the AFL's most likely first choice. Backers in Georgia had been after a franchise in both leagues for some time, but they were miffed with the NFL for their reticence to expand any sooner than 1967. Thus, the men of ink put their bets on Atlanta joining the AFL.

On Sunday, June 6, Buffalo Bills owner Ralph C. Wilson, Jr., told the *Buffalo Evening News* that merger talks between the leagues,

had been going on for three months."

The two leagues were ready to begin inter-league play on an exhibition basis in 1965, have a common draft of college players in the fall, and play a championship game in early 1966. Negotiations fell through over money. The AFL was to pay the NFL an indemnity. The owners expected to get the money through increased television revenues for inter-league play. Unfortunately, NBC, the AFL's broadcaster, wouldn't guarantee the extra money.

Merger discussions were reportedly going on among two AFL owners, who were not identified, and Carroll Rosenbloom, owner of the Baltimore Colts.

Pete Rozelle told reporters that there had been rumors of informal talks, but he believed the NFL's plans for expansion spoke for themselves. Joe Foss said he had been aware that various owners" had talked back and forth. Neither commissioner would say anything definite about a merger, although Foss predicted teams in both leagues would have their differences resolved eventually.

After deliberation and sifting through close to 60 applications from groups in 20 cities in the U.S. and Canada on June 7, the AFL owners voted unanimously to expand to a 10-team league for the 1966 season. An informal poll of owners indicated Atlanta and Philadelphia were running ahead of the field. Chicago and Milwaukee were right behind, and Detroit, Cleveland, New Orleans, Miami, and Los Angeles were still under consideration. Jets owner Sonny Werblin favored both Atlanta and Philadelphia because the league needed exposure in the Southeast and because Philly was one of the best sports cities in the country. Houston owner Bud Adams also supported Philadelphia and he wanted Atlanta, Miami or New Orleans because they are warm weather cities.

Unfortunately for the AFL owners, Rozelle wanted Atlanta in his league more than Foss did. Pete scheduled a meeting with Mayor Ivan Allen and members of the Atlanta Stadium Authority who had already made it known that they preferred an NFL franchise over one from the AFL. However, if Rozelle couldn't come up with anything concrete, then the mayor and the stadium people would accept an AFL franchise and only one from the new kids on the pro football block.

Rozelle went to Atlanta with dynamite in his pocket. He had taken a secret poll of the NFL owners the previous Friday. They voted 12-2 to expand into Atlanta in 1966 instead of waiting until 1967. At the same time, the AFL owners gave their stamp of approval to place a franchise in Atlanta to the Cox Broadcasting Company. Their deal had a catch issued by the AFL. The TV group had to find a suitable place to play its home games. With the ball now with Cox, they put a time limit on their offer. At the same time, the stadium group made it clear their decision on who would get the new facility would not be issued until July 1. This precluded the Cox group from getting the new stadium for an AFL team.

At the same time, a group of investors in Milwaukee made it clear that they would push as hard as they could to get an AFL team in the Cream City. Two questions needed the right answers in order for this to happen. The first—and simplest—was acceptance by the

AFL owners. Since the junior circuit had no franchises in the Midwest, the vote to award a spot in their league would most likely be unanimous. Now to the other question. Where would a Milwaukee team play its home games? Simple answer: County Stadium. But there was a fly in the ointment. William Anderson, manager of the facility, had *pledged sole use of the stadium for professional football* to none other than Vince Lombardi and his Green Bay Packers. Anderson said the pledge was actually a part of an ironclad contract. However, the stadium manager added it would allow an AFL team to come in … *if*—big word, if— *if* the Packers gave their permission to the AFL franchise. With a soft chuckle, Vince Lombardi allegedly said,

"Fat chance of that happening as long as the Packers are in the NFL."

Another consideration for a home field in Milwaukee was the unused stadium at Marquette University. It only seated 20,000, but that could be doubled by adding bleachers. In order to fill all those seats, the proposed AFL ownership suggested their team would play home games on Friday nights and Saturdays so as not to compete with the Packers for fans, especially when the Green & Gold was playing in County Stadium.

♦♦♦

The tug-of-war between the two leagues for accepting a bid to place a franchise in Atlanta came to a halt unofficially on June 11. Joe Foss made it clear the AFL wouldn't be able to keep its bid on the table until July 1. This left only the NFL to put a team in the Georgia capital. The question now? Which one of the three applicants would be awarded the franchise?

At the same time, the AFL's desire for a new member for its circuit to be in Philadelphia hit a brick wall. Just like Atlanta, the City of Brotherly Love was building a new football stadium. Occupancy was promised already to the Eagles. Foss and his owners still wished to put a team in Philly, but the owner of the Eagles had filed a lawsuit against the city to give them the exclusive right to play pro football in the new stadium. This move put a damper on the AFL's desire to get another team in the Northeast.

On June 22, the newspapers around the country reported that the NFL had declared a group headed by insurance magnate Rankin Smith, Jr., of Atlanta as the likely owner of a franchise in Atlanta. The Stadium Authority remained adamant that it wouldn't reveal which league would be offered the use of Atlanta's new stadium until July 1. Even so, everyone knew the mayor and the members of the Stadium Authority favored the NFL.

Joe Foss faced facts. He stated that the AFL had already given hope of landing franchises in both Atlanta and Philadelphia. However, he still had proposals from four other cities, one of them being New Orleans. Much to his dismay, Rozelle and the NFL were also high on getting a team in the Crescent City in 1967. Could the AFL win that battle? Time would tell.

In the meantime, Francis J. Schroedel, a building contractor from Milwaukee suburb Whitefish Bay, put in his own bid for an AFL franchise in the Cream City. Schroedel's attorney submitted letters to Milwaukee County officials and Father William F. Kelley, president of Marquette University, stating the construction magnate wanted to buy the Catholic college's football stadium and expand it, if possible. Both recipients of his offer withheld any immediate response.

Previously, Marvin L. Fishman, a realtor from Glendale, also a suburb of Milwaukee, had made his own bid for an AFL team to play in Milwaukee County Stadium, starting in 1968. County Chairman Eugene Grobschmidt stated quite unequivocally,

"I would do nothing to hurt the Packers."

Joe Foss stated the AFL had 61 other franchise requests from entrepreneurs representing cities from coast to coast. The league still planned to add two teams in 1966. Beyond that, only time would tell.

♦♦♦

On June 29th, NFL Commissioner Pete Rozelle made a truly historical announcement that was long overdue. The league was hiring five new game officials for the coming season. Not a big deal there except for the fact that one of them was a man of color. His name was Burl Abron Toler, a former San Francisco University star player. Toler was the very first person of color to become an official in any professional sport.

♦♦♦

Finally, on July 1, as promised, the Atlanta Stadium Authority made the announcement that it had awarded rights to the city's new 58,000 seat stadium to insurance magnate Rankin M. Smith. For the right to play in the NFL, Smith would pay the senior league an estimated $8 million that would be divided equally among its 14 current franchises. The Stadium Authority awarded Smith's entry into the NFL total playing rights for 10 years. For payment, the new franchise would pay the city 10 per cent of its gross admissions.

While gaining a decisive victory in Atlanta, the NFL also managed to keep its rival from obtaining playing rights to the planned $25 million stadium in Philadelphia. However, under a compromise agreement between the NFL Eagles and the city, the AFL obtained playing rights to the University of Pennsylvania's Franklin Field in 1967 when the new stadium would be completed. Lamar Hunt of the AFL expansion committee said he expected the league to delay moving into Philadelphia for a month or more because of the opposition of a few present owners. One of those owners was rumored to be Sonny Werblin of the New York Jets. Of course, this was only gossip because the Jets owner had stated earlier that Philadelphia was a great sports town and an AFL team there would be good for his Jets as well as the Patriots and Bills.

Meanwhile, with Atlanta now in the NFL bag, down in New Orleans promoter Dave Dixon said he had received a query about possible AFL expansion in 1966 into the Crescent City. As president of the New Orleans Pro Football Club, Inc., he announced that he would meet today with AFL officials to discuss the possibility of the junior league placing a team in his city. Despite his announcement of the AFL's interest in New Orleans, he said,

> ***"I think New Orleans should be the odds-on choice for the 16th NFL franchise."***

Dixon was the only enthusiast for the NFL to grant a franchise for the Louisiana city. Investment banker David H. McConnell, a New York millionaire, foamed at the mouth over possibly owning a team in New Orleans. He considered it to be a most excellent investment. So much so, that he flew down to Louisiana to meet with sportswriters first, then business and civic leaders in the city. From there, he drove up to Baton Rouge for a meeting with Louisiana's Governor John McKeithen, who had already pledged his assistance in the campaign to land a franchise in the expanding league. Next, he flew back to the Big Apple for a meeting with Pete Rozelle.

♦♦♦

Miami's City Commission took final steps on July 15 toward putting an American Football League team in the Orange Bowl in 1966. Their vote was unanimous for a letter of intent that would give the AFL an exclusive 60-day option to sign a contract with a franchise holder. Part of the proposal also included a reduction in the rent of the 75,000-seat stadium for the new team. The rent would be $150,000 for nine games for the first three years, then be increased gradually over the next two year.

AFL Commissioner Joe Foss said several groups were ready to buy a Miami franchise for around $7.5 million. That purchase money would be divvied up between the eight current teams and the league office.

Besides the windfall from a new team in Miami, advance ticket sales for the AFL were up 56.2 per cent. The advance sale of 935,606 tickets for the leagues 56 games surpassed the total paid attendance of the AFL's first season when the circuit's total turnout amounted to 927,216 fans. Season ticket sales amounted to 133,658 compared to 75,222 sales at the same time the year before.

Commissioner Foss said,

> ***"This is another yardstick by which the progress of the league can be measured." He***

> ***added, It indicates that our attendance, which was up 16 per cent last year (over the 1963 campaign), will be up by even a higher percentage this year."***

In short, the AFL was gaining more popularity by the year and putting it on a sound footing equal to the NFL. Bigger television deals, fatter contracts for players, and paid attendance signaled success by the five-year-old league. So, what was next for the two pro circuits? A mutual draft? More expansion? Merger? All three seemed inevitable.

♦♦♦

Being thwarted by the NFL to land a team in Atlanta, the moguls of the AFL turned their attention to Miami. They presented their terms for a franchise to be placed in the Florida city.

> ***"We have indicated we want to go there," Milt Woodard, the assistant AFL commissioner, said today. But the move would be contingent upon the new franchise-holder contracting with the city of Miami for the Orange Bowl. If they will (sic) negotiate a fair lease, we will go to Miami."***

The path to the deepest south apparently cleared by Joe Foss the week before when he met with Miami city officials. He worked out verbally a long-term agreement for the use of the Orange Bowl, but the final contract must be drawn up with the new franchise-holder, whoever he or they may be.

Besides a formal agreement on a contract, the man or group that wins the franchise would have to pay the AFL 7.5 million bucks to be in the younger league. This money would be split up equally by the eight existing teams and the league's home office.

This was all well and good – initially. Some owners were against placing a team in Miami. Why? Miami was a far piece of real estate away from every single one of the other cities in the AFL. San Diego and Oakland? All the way across the country to the west coast. Denver, Houston, and Kansas City? Closer but still hours away from

Miami, if even by air. New York, Buffalo, and Boston? Farther away from the Florida city than Houston, the closest city, a whole 900 miles away in a straight line.

♦♦♦

In the meantime, Roy Hofheinz, president of the Houston Astros National League team, made it known that he wanted to head up an NFL franchise and have it play its home games in the brand-spanking new Astrodome. This was contingent on him succeeding in purchasing 53% of the Astro stock owned by R.E. (Bob) Smith, board chairman and oil millionaire.

There was also the minor fact that the owners of the NFL wanted to put a team in Houston to compete against the AFL Oilers. This possibility was highly unlikely, considering the fact that the rival league team had become deeply entrenched in the Texas city. Besides that, the NFL owners were already secretly intending on placing a franchise in New Orleans; if not in 1966, then in 1967. No matter what the AFL tried to do, the NFL aimed to thwart the upstart league in its expansion desires.

Hofheinz finally got his way with Smith and obtained 83% of the stock in the Astros and their home field. However, he lost his first football tenant in the Astrodome when the Oilers owner Bud Adams bailed on him and made a deal to play his team's home games in the 70,000 seat Rice University Stadium for the next five years.

Hofheinz, the real estate tycoon, would do his damnedest to get an NFL team. He invited NFL Commissioner Pete Rozelle to pay a visit to Houston and look over the Astrodome. Rozelle said the fact that Houston already had a team in the AFL would not affect the NFL's decision to locate a franchise there.

> ***"They've been in four of our cities," said Rozelle. We'll move into whatever city is in the best interest of our league, and I am sure they feel the same way about placing a franchise in an NFL city. After all, Dallas, St. Louis, and Pittsburgh should be very embarrassed. They are the only cities that***

haven't been named as possible sites for AFL franchises."

Rozelle then mentioned a list of prospective cities for the NFL to consider for expansion. Toronto, Montreal, Boston Miami, New Orleans, Houston, Seattle, Portland, Phoenix, and Cincinnati would be researched by a marketing company before a short list was handed to the NFL owners to consider for team number 16.

That was the plan until the AFL started raiding the NFL for some of its best players.

♦♦♦

Finally, on August 16, AFL Commissioner Joe Foss announced that his league had granted a group headed by comedian and television star Danny Thomas a five-year franchise for a ninth team in Miami. Thomas quipped,

"You can't show me any Lebanese boy raised in Toledo, Ohio, who didn't want to own a Miami ball club."

Thus far, a name for the new team had not yet been decided on. The Miami club would play seven home games in the Orange Bowl beginning in 1966. Thomas's partner was Joe Robbie, a lawyer from Minneapolis. They agreed to take in other stockholders later. Thomas said his part in managing the franchise would depend on his television filming schedule.

To stock the team with veteran players, Foss said the player limit of 36 this season would be raised to 38. For the player draft, he announced each team would put together a list of 23 players that would be protected from being drafted by Miami. The new club would then be allowed to select two players from each team, then one more player would be protected from going to Miami. Then the new team could select two more players from each team, giving them a roster of 32 veteran players.

Miami would then get to pick two players from the college draft and the first pick in each succeeding round.

This was a good deal for Miami. Besides getting four seasoned players from each team, the new franchise would receive two shots at obtaining the services of the best pair of college players in the country. In the second round, Miami would pick the #11 player coming out of college that winter. That's three of the top 11 players, followed by the 20th and 29th. If the fledgling organization was lucky, it would give it an open door at obtaining five of the best 29 players in the country. Of course, this was always only a possibility, not a certainty. At the time, anything could happen in pro football.

As usual, when one league made news in the press, the other league would counter with a story of its own. In this case, Pete Rozelle, commissioner of the NFL, posted his own piece on the future of his league.

Rozelle jumped two years into the future when he declared the NFL would expand to 16 teams by 1967. Rozelle added news that the league would remain a two-conference league of eight teams each. Then the two division winners would play for the conference title. This round would be followed by the NFL title game.

There was no mention of a game between the NFL and AFL champions to declare one king of the two major leagues. Neither Foss nor Rozelle wanted to speculate on a super title game" between their respective champions. Too early for that, we should surmise.

♦♦♦

At their opening meeting in mid-September, the AFL owners voted to expand their league to 10 teams in 1967 and indicated they would add two more teams in 1968 and 1969. The 10th team would most likely be selected from among Chicago, Los Angeles, New Orleans, Milwaukee, and Washington, Commissioner Joe Foss told reporters after the owners meeting in Houston.

> ***"The sentiment I got from the owners," Foss said, was we can go to 12 teams. Expansion beyond the 10th team definitely is contemplated."***

Some remarkably interesting facts about Joe Foss and co-owner Joe Robbie of the first expansion city . Both men were members of the South Dakota legislature in 1950. Foss sought the Republican nomination for governor that year but lost. Robbie received the Democratic nomination that year but was defeated in the general election. Foss was elected governor four years later.

The AFL commissioner declined to say when the 10th city would be named, but he did say it might be named at the annual meeting after the 1965 season. He added that the 10th team would be given the first two selections in the 1st Round of the 1966 college draft and the first selection in each succeeding round. In addition to the cream of the draft, the 10th club would be permitted to draft four players from each of the current clubs. Miami would be exempted. The other teams would be allowed to protect only 23 players each.

This was a nice plan for expansion, one that the owners in the NFL eyed with great concern.

♦♦♦

On November 2, NFL Commissioner Pete Rozelle urged Chicagoans to put on an all-out effort for a new football stadium to be built in their city or at least in a suburb. While discussing some dozen cities which have already or planned to have by the next year, Rozelle said the Bears in 1966 would be playing in the smallest and most antiquated arena in the country.

On the subject of expansion for 1967, Rozelle named six cities that were being considered for the 16th team. That list included four cities that had never been mentioned before. Those cities were Boston, Portland, Phoenix, and Cincinnati. Previously named as possible cities for expansion were New Orleans and Houston.

The Arizona capital made the list because it and its several suburbs in Maricopa County were the fastest growing area in the country with a population that had recently boomed from a little less than a quarter of a million people in 1950 to three times that number in 1965. Besides the number of people living in Phoenix and its immediate surroundings the year round, the Valley of the Sun was a known winter residence for retired people who were politely known as "Snowbirds" and folks who were laid off from their regular jobs because of the cold and snow in northern parts of the country. Already, people in Phoenix were talking about landing an expansion franchise in professional basketball and hockey. So why not a football team?

♦♦♦

A few days later another rumor made the newspapers. The headline read:

AFL Franchise Headed for Los Angeles, Paper Reports

The newspaper was the LA *Herald-Examiner*, but the source of the story was the *Associated Press.* Of course, there was no credit for the report. Whoever wrote the piece stated the AFL would be putting a franchise either in Dodger Stadium in Los Angeles or in the new park being built in Anaheim. One or the other would happen in 1967, and either would depend on financial arrangements.

Kansas City Chiefs owner Lamar Hunt will get first chance to move his club to the West Coast, but if he didn't want to move, then the league would probably place an expansion team there. Contacted at his home in Dallas, Hunt said he had no interest in moving his team anywhere. He even denied knowing anything about the rumor, but he did admit that the AFL owners were interested in either Los Angeles or Orange County. He further admitted that some people had talked to him about moving the Chiefs, but again he denied having any true interest in moving his franchise.

Later that week AP writer Ben Thomas reported a huge move by the city of New Orleans. The announcement of plans for a domed stadium was made official by Mayor Victor H. Schiro.

After the word went out that the city planned to build a $24-million super-dome stadium, an NFL spokesman in New York said the availability of the proposed stadium would weigh heavily in New Orleans' favor in the granting of a franchise for the city.

> ***"Currently, we are having research conducted by an independent firm in seven cities, one of which is New Orleans," said the spokesman. He added, And certainly one of the major considerations in its study will be the availability of suitable stadiums. Construction of such a stadium in New Orleans would be in its favor, as it would any of the other six."***

The NFL had already said it would grant a franchise for a 16th team—to begin playing in the 1967 season—sometime next spring. The story continued by naming the same cities Pete Rozelle had said were under consideration two days before. What it didn't state was now New Orleans was at the top of the list.

♦♦♦

On November 11, the AFL Commissioner Joe Foss dropped a major bomb on college football. He announced that the AFL would be holding its draft of college players on November 20.

Of course, this announcement absolutely incensed the college football coaches, athletic directors, and other officials. Why? Because their football seasons went well beyond November 20. If they were drafted and offered a pile of money to sign a contract, these players would become ineligible to play in college bowl games. The same anger was fired at the Pro Leagues the year before. They raged over alleged secret drafts, player-hiding, early signings, and double signings.

The year before the two major pro football leagues told the National Collegiate Athletic Association that they would refrain from signing players before their college eligibility had ended. Also, the NCAA asked that the drafts be held no earlier than November 27, the last big Saturday of college football.

Foss explained why the AFL picked November 20 as their draft day.

> ***"First, it is the day on which a majority of college teams complete their schedules. And, further, I personally feel that drafting on the 20th will go a long way toward eliminating so-called baby-sitting practices which have sprung up the last two years." He explained what he meant by baby-sitting practices."***

> ***"A number of unsavory situations came to light from the practice of players being hidden away for several days prior to the last two drafts. I think it's in the best interest of all***

> ***that we do our best to try and eliminate an increasingly unhealthy situation."***

James Corbett of Louisiana State and chairman of the NCAA committee on pro football relations didn't take the same view.

> ***"The AFL action makes a mockery of that league's agreement with the NCAA and its member colleges. A draft as early as November 20 can only be a completely negative morale factor since there will be increased pressure on the drafted player, on his team, and on his college—at exactly the wrong time."***

Foss said the AFL would not violate the NCAA's primary concern over early signings.

> ***"We just want a chance to contact the players and make our sales pitch. We understand the NFL has made elaborate plans again for babysitting with prospects, and we want to get the chance to talk to those prospects."***

NFL Commissioner Pete Rozelle didn't say anything about the babysitting charges, but he did say the league tentatively was planning its draft for November 27:

> ***"in accordance with the wishes of colleges and universities. However, we may be forced to draft much sooner if others fail to honor requests."***

The two leagues continued to battle. How far away was peace? Only time had yet to tell.

♦♦♦

A good sign that a merger between the two major professional football leagues wasn't all that far into the future hit the newspapers on Tuesday, November 16, 1965. An item coming out of San Diego headlined:

> ***Citizens Plump For Ram-Charger Exhibition in '67***
>
> ***"A citizens campaign was launched Monday to pit the National Football League Los Angeles Rams against the San Diego Chargers in an exhibition game in 1967.***
>
> ***The notable inter-city rivalry" would dedicate San Diego's new 50,000 seat stadium.***

Albert Harutunian, Jr., chairman of the Citizens Stadium Committee, said in a telegram to Rams President Dan Reeves, Jr.:

> ***"This is your opportunity to rise above petty inter-league jealousies and share in progress of all Southern California," the telegram said."***
>
> ***Dan Reeves had yet to reply.***

The very next day the AFL announced it would have its draft on the same day as the NFL. This was just another baby step in the right direction toward a merger of the two leagues.

♦♦♦

In a major *Associated Press* story on Thanksgiving Day in the Green Bay *Press-Gazette*, the feces really hit the pro football fan, the maker of wind, not the sports follower.

A Dallas, Texas newspaper, claimed that a much-denied secret draft staged by the AFL owners had given the young circuit a:

> ***"big jump in the contract battle with the rival NFL."***

The author of this story was one Steve Perkins, a very gifted sportswriter known for his drinking, his unusually large and oddly shaped nose, and his embroidery of the facts in his sports coverage. Perkins wrote,

> ***"With 'first rights' assigned to individual clubs after six rounds of selections in their New York meeting, the AFL teams have been able to contact top collegians this week and offer them cash terms ... They are telling the boys, 'we've got you, so put your name right here."***

The story quoted *a National Football League recruiter as saying. (Author's italics.)* A National Football League *recruiter*? NFL teams had scouts, not recruiters, ever since Curly Lambeau came up with the idea of having a draft.

> ***"The Times Herald last week gave details of the alleged early draft and named nine players chosen. Several AFL owners hotly denied any such meeting. But Denver owner Gerald Phipps said the clubs chose top players and said next Saturday's official draft would follow along the same lines." (Author's italics again.)***

A draft list came next, team by team, starting with the New York Jets and including the Miami Dolphins.

The *Times Herald* was known for its yellow journalism. That was what made it popular in Texas whose citizens have always relished tall tales of all kinds.

♦♦♦

The war between the two major professional leagues would continue into the following year, starting with the college draft on the Saturday after Thanksgiving 1965, which is the beginning of the next volume of *The History of the Green Bay Packers: Lombardi's Destiny, Part 4.*

§ § §

3

Vince Vows Victory

Rumors clouded the horizon for the Packers as the New Year shifted into gear. The first of these concerned Paul Hornung.

Charles Feeney of the New York *Journal-American* started all the claptrap about Hornung. He wrote that Paul was finished with the Packers and might be traded to the New York Giants. Feeney's article also had Lombardi and the Golden Boy reaching the breaking point in their coach-player relationship when the team was in Miami preparing for the Playoff Bowl with the St. Louis Cardinals. According to the Big Apple sportswriter, Hornung had been late for a team meeting and had called Lombardi to apologize, to which the coach barked at him, Get in your car and keep going."

> ***"There's no truth to it," Lombardi told Art Daley. It's a lie."***

Lombardi had always said that he would make any trade, if he thought it would help the team. He added that, if Hornung desired a trade, he would have to initiate it himself, it would have to come from Hornung.

The coach added:

> ***"I don't know a player in the National Football League who has the potential of Hornung. You don't give up something for nothing. Now I'm not saying that we're going to stand pat. If we have an opportunity to***

> ***better ourselves, we will trade. But I have no plans to trade Hornung, period."***

Hornung said:

> ***"This is the first I've heard of such reports. I'm perfectly happy in Green Bay. And any reports that I have not been getting along with Coach Lombardi are untrue."***

♦♦♦

Besides signing a rookie here and there in December of 1964 and in early January of the New Year, Lombardi made a major trade. Looking back on the 1964 season and beyond, Vince realized that having his regulars doing double duty as kickers, such as Hornung kicking PATs and field goals, was no longer a good idea. Instead, he decided to follow the examples of the Cleveland Browns and New York Giants and use a specialist to do the placekicking for points and kickoffs. If one could be found, a man who could also do the punting would be ideal. He looked around and found the perfect man for the job. The only problem was the guy that he wanted was playing for another team. Fortunately for Vince, the prize he sought played for his old friends in New York. The Maras were always willing to deal with their old school chum—if the price was right.

Lombardi dangled a draft choice in front of the Maras for their kicker. Don Chandler was a 5th Round choice for the Giants in 1956. He was 30 years old and would be 31 at the beginning of the next season. An additional 5th Round pick in the 1966 draft would be good for the aging Giants. The deal was done. Chandler for a single draft pick.

No longer would Hornung and Jerry Kramer kick extra points and field goals for the Packers. Lee Roy Caffey would be a backup on kickoffs, and Jerry Norton would be out of a job as the team's punter. Or so it seemed in January. Training camp might make a difference for everybody involved in the kicking game.

A rumor circulated among the media that Hornung was part of the trade with the Giants. The Golden Boy for Chandler straight up. Hornung remarked that he would love to play in New York. Lombardi denied the story as quickly as it appeared in the newspapers. Hornung doused the rumor fire with a few words of his own.

> ***"... a National Football League player is like a chattel. You can be bought and sold. Lombardi is a good man, strong and respected. I know that if he did deal me, it would be for the good of his team and for me. That's the kind of man he is."***

When asked how he would like to be a six-figure bonus baby like Namath and Huarte, Hornung laughed and said,

> ***"I'd be looking for seven figures."***

> ***"Then he added, The game has been very good to me. I don't resent the college kids getting all that money. In fact, it puts the established players in a better bargaining position."***

When he was told that the Dallas Cowboys had roped and hog-tied Malcolm Walker, linebacker from Rice, with a unique $80,000 deposit in a savings account in his name, Hornung laughed again and said,

> ***"That wouldn't be for me. I'd take the whole 80 thousand and run off to Paris. They would have to address me: Paul Hornung, Left Bank."***

Hornung remained a Packer, but much to everyone's surprise, Bill Austin resigned his post as offensive line coach for Green Bay. He had been coaching the best O-line in the NFL since 1959. He cited his reason for leaving was his wife's health. Apparently, she was allergic to cold weather and needed to live in a warmer climate. Austin found one for her when he signed on with the Los Angeles Rams as their new line coach, replacing Ray Wietecha who had resigned the week before.

Oddly enough, Lombardi turned around and hired Wietecha as the Packers' new offensive line coach. Wietecha played 10 years for the New York Giants, half of them under Lombardi when he was with the New Yorkers as their offensive coach.

At the same time, Ron Kramer was rumored to be wanting out of Green Bay to go play for the Lions. He cited family reasons. His son had suffered a freak eye injury in 1964 and had to have surgery on it in a Detroit hospital. Another surgery was in the offing, so Kramer felt the necessity of being with his family in the Motor City. Ron's teammate, Jerry Kramer, said later,

> ***"He asked Coach Lombardi to trade him (Ron) because he was trying to save his marriage."***

Reportedly, Ron Kramer played out his contract option" with Green Bay and was saying he would not play for any team other than the Detroit Lions. Lombardi refused to surrender the Packers' right to Kramer. He said, if Ron should sign a deal with any other NFL team, then he would demand compensation of equal value.

League rules stipulated that when a player plays out his option and subsequently signs with another team, then his new team must compensate his old club with a player of comparable value. In this case, Detroit tendered their first choice in the following year's draft. NFL Commissioner Pete Rozelle approved of this transaction, although Lombardi stated, The decision of the commissioner that Ron Kramer be awarded to Detroit in return for a draft choice is under no circumstances to be understood to be a trade, but rather a decision by the commissioner."

Kramer was overjoyed by the deal. So was Marv Fleming who was considered to become big Ron's replacement at tight end.

♦♦♦

On President Lincoln's birthday, General Manager Vince Lombardi revealed some good news for Packer fans who had their names on the season ticket applicants list. The Packers were investing in more seats for City Stadium. How many more? Over eight thousand! This would bring the stadium's capacity to 50,500, almost room enough for two-thirds of the population of little Green Bay."

In addition to the seating increase, the Packers chose to expand the Administration Building by adding two one-story wings, both fronting 1265 Highland Avenue (now Lombardi Avenue), and a tunnel 190-feet long from the players dressing rooms to the north end of the Stadium. The cost of construction would be $500,000, every dollar coming from Green Bay Packers, Inc.

Lombardi was alleged to have been opposed to spending the money for this expansion, saying, We'll never fill it." This is hard to believe, considering the number of ticket requests made each year. Of course, Vince was *alleged* to have said a lot of things that simply weren't true or were twisted.

♦♦♦

After three months of all quiet on the western front" in the NFL, the Packers made a major trade. Lombardi sent veteran linebacker Dan Currie to the Los Angeles Rams for fleet-footed receiver Carroll Dale. With the Packers for seven years, Currie would be 30 before the 1965 season began, while Dale would be 27. A veteran of five seasons on the West Coast Dale was drafted out of Virginia Tech in the 8th Round of the 1959 Draft as a future. So far in his career the speedy pass catcher had hauled in 149 aerials for 2,663 yards and 17 touchdowns. Dale was considered to be a deep threat, something the Packers had been lacking for the past few seasons.

♦♦♦

The *Press-Gazette* headline said it all:

Packers Made Record $404,730 Profit In '64

The huge difference from year-to-year came directly from the increase in television revenue. This signaled the financial future for the Packers would always be in the black.

General Manager Vince Lombardi revealed the situation for ticket sales.

> ***"In Green Bay, new season ticket orders have totaled 13,127, and old holders have asked for 2,204 season tickets, making a total of 15,331.***

> *While the capacity of City Stadium has been jumped to 50,800, the 8,500 added seats won't handle the requests. There was a total of 42,251 season ticket renewals from last year, and only 76 were not returning due to deaths or people moving out of the city. The season tickets here are held by more than 11,000 persons."*
>
> *Milwaukee is sold out on season tickets, although 2,000 seats will be sold on a single game basis August 16. We already have a waiting list of 813 for our 1966 games in Milwaukee. The Milwaukee seats are held by 6,713 persons, and it's interesting to note that only 122 are from Green Bay and DePere.*
>
> *The response has been excellent for the Shriner's game in Milwaukee and the other two pre-season games. The Shriner's game was scheduled in the afternoon at the request of the Shriner's and not at the request of CBS."*

Lombardi summed up his remarks.

> *"Our stadium here has always been major league from the standpoint of beauty, availability, parking, and for the fans and the teams. With more seats, more people will get a chance to see the Packers, and the visiting teams will receive more income. This, we can all be proud of."*

Again, this hardly sounds like a man who boo-hooed expansion of the stadium, saying, *"We'll never fill it."* Of course, the man who told this author this bit of gossip was under the influence of several mixed drinks at the time.

♦♦♦

Jerry Kramer missed several games during the 1964 season, due to an infected abscess in his abdomen that was removed by surgery. He had to have another operation in May the next year to remove the cause of the pustule.

> ***"You know what?" Kramer said to Art Daley after the six and a half hours procedure. He (the surgeon) took out three pieces of wood out of my groin. They'd been in there for 11 and a half years. Just think. He (the surgeon) took out three slivers of wood, but they were bigger than slivers. "Two of them were four inches long and about a half-inch around, and the other was two inches long. They were imbedded in my groin since I was 17 years old. The wood didn't show up in the X-rays anywhere, but he (the surgeon) dug around there and found them."***

Kramer's illness resulted from what was termed a barnyard infection" that was apparently caused by the wood that became stuck in his groin during an accident near his home in Idaho.

> ***"I was chasing this calf and running as hard as I could when the calf stepped on a leaning board. The board splintered and stuck me in the groin as I fell on the sharp end. I laid down, and they pulled some of the slivers out of me, but a few days later they removed some of the board from my back. It had gone clean through, and we know now that some of it stayed right in me."***

Those three pieces of wood?

Kramer hooted a chuckle.

> ***"I guess they're the finest souvenirs I ever had. They'll go into my collection."***

Besides the calf incident, Kramer had part of an arm shot off in a hunting accident and was nearly killed when he was shot in one side by a 10-gauge shotgun when he was a kid.

Kramer termed himself to be:

> ***"the unluckiest, luckiest guy in the world."***

♦♦♦

Paul Orndorff, a writer for *United Press International* wrote an article about Packer Paul Hornung and his future with Green Bay. He ended the piece by mentioning Hornung was about to become an author. The book had yet to be released, and the Golden Boy refused to reveal the title of his tome.

> ***"I'm not going to say anything about it until it is released for publication."***

Orndorff assured his readers that the book was certain to contain the often-repeated tale that Hornung told after the Packers' second loss to the Colts in 1964.

> ***"A Packer fan slipped a gun into my head gear as I was walking to the dressing room. Apparently, he wanted me to use it on myself. I sat and thought about it, then took the gun out and pointed it to my head. About that time Bart Starr came running across the room yelling, 'Paul, have you gone crazy?' Jim Taylor simply said, 'Ah, let him go. He'll miss'."***

Taylor was referring to Hornung's number of missed field goals and PATs in those two games, both losses that cost the Packers another division title and a shot at the NFL title.

♦♦♦

++In mid-June, Lombardi stated that in spite of what the doctors said, he doubted Jerry Kramer would play in the coming season. At a banquet in Menasha, a city upriver from Green Bay, Kramer said the doctors said his stomach wall would be stronger than ever because of the scar tissue created by the surgery to remove the sticks from his abdomen and from his upcoming hernia operation. He further stated he just might be ready for the beginning of practice in July.

♦♦♦

*Press-Gazette*s sports editor Art Daley wrote a piece about the rookies who would begin practice drills on Wednesday, July 21. The 25-man roster included three quarterbacks, nine halfbacks, one fullback, three ends, six tackles, two guards, one center who also played linebacker. Of the half dozen tackles, four were draftees and the other two were free agents.

Lombardi picked 25 players in the draft back in December. Only 11 of those selected signed with the Packers. Five selections put their signatures on AFL contracts. Eight were future picks for the 1966 season. One passed on football and signed a baseball deal.

For camp, the coach had 11 free agents and three futures from the year before to go along with his 11 draft picks from the latest draft. Just enough bodies for his veterans to scrimmage against once they arrived on the 25th.

♦♦♦

Despite the increase in seating in City Stadium, which was over 3,000 more seats than Milwaukee County Stadium, fans holding Green Bay season tickets were not pressuring Lombardi or the corporation's officers for more games to be played in the parent city. So said the general manager on a statewide network television program aired on July 12. The general manager stated, We will continue to play the same number of games in Milwaukee and add an extra pre-season game there next year."

When asked about the coming season, Coach Lombardi said in complete confidence,

"We will win it."

He meant the NFL title.

> ***"What we need most (this season) is defensive help, despite having led the league there last year. We will have the biggest crop of rookies, in both size and number, than we have ever had. Bill Curry (rookie from Georgia Tech) will be tried at both center and linebacker. It looks like he could help us. At least four or five other clubs would like to have him. They've been calling me."***

Lombardi then confessed to being approached by a group of investors in Philadelphia to be their coach and general manager of an AFL team, should one be placed there. He responded that he wasn't interested in accepting their proposition at the present time. The Packers GM then revealed he had not been approached by anyone from Milwaukee about sharing County Stadium with the Pack. Contact or not, Lombardi wasn't about to share access to County Stadium with any team from another league. In his mind, the Packers weren't just a Green Bay team; the Pack was a Wisconsin team.

§ § §

4

Good-bye, Curly Lambeau, Sorry to See You Go

On April 23, 1965, *Press-Gazette* sportswriter Lee Remmel wrote a piece about Curly Lambeau in his daily column, *Personality Parade.* No one thought at the time this might be the last hurrah for the legendary leader who was the center focus of pro football in Green Bay for 31 years.

Curly had just returned from wintering in fabulous Palm Springs, California. Remmel remarked on that, then he gave Lambeau the credit he deserved for the Packers playing a portion of their home schedule in Milwaukee, starting back in 1933. Curly's key remark about that was the Packers would always play in Milwaukee because they belonged to the citizens of Wisconsin, not just Green Bay, and playing the entire schedule in Green Bay would cost them fans in the long run. He added that a team in Milwaukee from another league, such as the AFL or the new Continental Football League (COFL), that was successful on the field would undoubtedly be adopted by the hometown fans and make it financially viable.

Since no real competitor has yet to be placed in the Cream City since World War II or is likely to be put in Milwaukee, we may never know if Curly was right or wrong with his opinion.

Then Remmel changed the topic of their conversation to the present, meaning the conflict between the NFL and AFL. Remmel asked Lambeau if he could foresee an early peace between the two now established circuits. They might play each other someday, but I hope they don't— it would be quite lopsided. The AFL is not in a class with the NFL. They have some good backs, but they don't have the overall coaching or the offensive or defensive personnel.

Remmel's next question concerned the possibility of a title game between the two league champions.

> ***"It's not for me to say, but I can't see it for quite a while. What for? They're playing football in the middle of January now. What will it prove? It probably will come, but the AFL has to improve more."***

Lambeau then postulated on the current quality of play in pro football, meaning the NFL.

> ***"It's a better game today than when we won three championships back in '29, '30, and '31, largely because of free substitution. It's more specialized, and there are more good players, and the players are bigger. It's faster, too, because the fellows are fresher because they play only one way and they give you better football.***
>
> ***TV has given it a tremendous lift, too. The game had to be successful—it was natural, but TV got a lot more people interested. It made more fans. Here was something pretty good—you just had to have more people see it."***

Remmel concluded his column with some of Lambeau's NFL accomplishments, including a comparison of players from his era to those of the game in the 1960s. He ended the piece with Curly's second favorite subject: his golf game. Curly boasted about regularly shooting in the 80s. Lambeau's final quip, *"Pretty good for a young kid."*

Three nights later Lambeau made his last public appearance at the annual Elks Club's Sports Dinner. Curly and five men who had played for him were now being honored as part of the first two classes of the Pro Football Hall of Fame. They were Mike Michalske, Don Hutson, Cal Hubbard, Clark Hinkle, and Johnny (Blood) McNally.

Dignitaries abounded that evening, speaking in turn. Richard McCann, director of the Pro Football Hall of Fame in Canton, Ohio, the principal speaker; Oliver Kuechle, sports editor of the *Milwaukee Journal*; Packer president Dominic Olejniczak; and toastmaster Lloyd Larson, sports editor of the *Milwaukee Sentinel*, all of whom witnessed the development of the NFL from its tottering infant stage into its current state in 1965. After all of them groped the podium for several minutes each, the master of speechmakers Vince Lombardi stepped up to the microphone.

> ***"With all due respect to my friend Curly, I think I could have done a pretty good job of coaching these fellows myself."***

Lombardi directed a sly grin right at Lambeau, seated a few feet to his left. His remark brought a collective round of chuckles from the audience of nearly 500 diners, including Curly, although his titter was a bit forced, while the rest were more to the wry side, especially those by the five other men being honored that night. Those who had played for Lambeau knew him to be a hard taskmaster when drilling the team in practice, but a weak decision maker when it came to actual combat on the field. An example of this happened in a game in 1929.

The Packers on the field weren't playing up to Curly's desire, so he inserted himself into the game, saying, I'll show them how to run with the ball." He called his own number in the huddle, which brought on a round of rolling eyes from the other 10 men. Red Dunn took the snap and handed off to Lambeau. The Packer linemen made little effort to block their opponents, allowing them to break through with ease and smash Curly in the backfield. Lambeau struggled to get up, and when he did, he wobbled back to the bench, plopped down, and never played another down, ending his career as a player right then and there. Dunn was the real mastermind of the Packers winning three straight titles, although Lambeau was given credit for the feat in spite of the fact in those days the quarterback called the plays because the coaches on the sidelines were not allowed by rule to send in plays.

Lombardi called Curly his friend in public, but in private he voiced his disdain for this man of a lesser intellect. Vince continued,

> ***"Here is a man who has coached five Hall of Fame members. I don't think anybody will ever break that record."***

Lombardi probably knew that several of his current players were already among the greats of all time and would one day be inducted into the Hall. Lambeau's list was added to in time with Tony Canadeo, Arnie Herber, and Walt Kiesling, giving him eight inductees during his 28 years as Green Bay's head coach. Lombardi's list would include Herb Adderley, Willie Davis, Bobby Dillon, Forrest Gregg, Paul Hornung, Henry Jordan, Jerry Kramer, Ray Nitschke, Jim Ringo, Dave Robinson, Bart Starr, Jim Taylor, Emlen Tunnell, and Willie Wood, a total of 14 over nine years as the man in charge of the Packers.

Little did Lambeau or anyone else know that this would be his final interview.

Earl Louis Curly" Lambeau died suddenly from a heart attack at 7:30 p.m. Tuesday, June 2, 1965 at a private home in Sturgeon Bay. The Packer corporation and the state media immortalized him with their coverage of his death and funeral. They made him appear to be bigger than life, a real sports hero, if there ever was one. For decades, they had done this. But why? Let's check the facts about Curly, his family, and some of the people who were part and parcel in his early life in Green Bay.

♦♦♦

Earl Louis Curly" Lambeau was born April 9, 1898 in Green Bay, Wisconsin, the son of Marcelin Marcel" and Mary LaTour Lambeau.

Curly's father was born October 9, 1876 in Green Bay, Wisconsin, the son of Victor Lambeau, a Belgian immigrant by way of Canada. Marcel worked as a mason initially, then became a building contractor. When he was a boy, Marcel behaved very badly and was sent away to the Waukesha Reform School, where he was incarcerated for two years and three months before being released in January 1888 for good behavior. Had he learned his lesson? Not really. He only learned how to control his anger and use it at the right times as time would tell.

Having worked as a mason in his teen years, Marcel Lambeau continued in his father's line of work as a member of the Bricklayers and Masons Union. He rose to the position of vice-president of the union in 1902. At the same, he owned a saloon on Main Street, and a year later he purchased a boarding house that he expanded to accommodate 20 boarders. Just before Christmas 1904, he was elected president of the local Masons Union. In 1906, he was elected captain of the union's baseball team. That same year the unions banded together to form the Building Trades Council, and Marcel was elected temporary president. December 24, 1908, Marcel was elected president of the Brewers Union. All of these offices did not gain him wealth, they gave him power and political punch. In a nutshell, he was a very, very important citizen in and around Green Bay.

Newspapers in the 19th Century and early 20th Century were known for withholding the names of their advertisers and other very prominent persons in their community when they did something that might appear to be scandalous. When they couldn't withhold their names, the newsmen would alter the person's first name or surname or both. In Marcel's case, an item about a Michael" Lambeau forging a check appeared in the *Press-Gazette* appeared on September 23, 1901. Another instance of this practice made the paper when a certain Marsh" Lambeau pled guilty to assault and battery on one Eugene Ducat and paid a fine of a dollar and court costs of $6.56.

Marcel's father was Victor Joseph Lambeau, born August 14, 1853. He immigrated to the United States by way of Canada in 1873 and was naturalized in 1889 in Green Bay, Brown County, Wisconsin. Victor's occupation was mason, and he and his partner built many very prominent buildings in Green Bay. He was very well respected in the community until October 5, 1891 when he met up with his wife Marie Adolphine on a street corner in downtown Green Bay. The couple argued briefly before the husband pulled a .32-caliber revolver and shot her through the neck. As soon as she fell to the sidewalk, he put the gun to his right temple and killed himself. Several people witnessed the attempted murder and the subsequent suicide. Seeing that the wife was still alive, although bleeding profusely, a few onlookers came to her aid and got her to a hospital where the doctor saved her life. Why did Victor commit this horrible misdeed? Many of his associates stated to the coroner's jury that he had suspected his wife of infidelity. Of course, such a suspicion would enrage most husbands. It carried poor Victor completely over the edge.

Curly's mother's maiden name was LaTour. Both of his parents were children of Belgian immigrants. After Curly, came three siblings: Raymond Emil Rummy" born May 5, 1900; Oliver Dewey Ollie" born April 1, 1902; and Beatrice born May 23, 1904. Another daughter was born to the Lambeaus per the Birth Record published in the *Press-Gazette* on May 22, 1906. Sadly, she passed in childhood.

The first mention of Curly in the *Press-Gazette* was printed in the March 28, 1911 edition. A short, one-sentence item in the gossip column told he had returned home from Sheboygan after spending a week there with friends.

Curly's name next appeared on June 18, 1913 in the pages of the *Press-Gazette* when the paper printed a piece about the graduating class of Howe School. He had been student body president that past school year. Already, his popularity and leadership qualities had attained the social pinnacle among his peers. Those friends and relatives closest to him recognized then that he just might be headed to great heights.

In the fall, Curly became a freshman at Green Bay East High School. Only his surname appeared in the newspaper on October 6, 1913. Lambeau carried the ball over the line and (Joseph) Martin kicked goal." Curly was a freshman that year, and already he was leading his team in scoring. The game with Shawano High ended in a 7-all tie. With the exception of the game rosters in the paper, Curly was not mentioned again until May 29, 1914 when he took part in a debate at East High. Naturally, he and his partner won the contest, proving he was already quite a talker, a trait that would serve him well right up to the very end of his life.

Curly's next mention in the *Press-Gazette* came in his sophomore year September 25, 1914 in an article about the East High football team's first game of the season. In the first four paragraphs of the story, the writer praised the East team for its spectacular play in their 66-0 victory over DePere High. All but one of Green Bay's players were acknowledged by their surnames, but I have found some of their given names. Among them were Dominic Francis Frank" Flatley and Joseph Joe" Martin (tackles), William C. Wittig (halfback), Frank Anton Binish (fullback), and Francis John Frank" Van Laanen (quarterback), Frank Jenske and Casey Loomis ends. Coach Carroll Nelson also found his moniker in print.

The next week Curly's team added real insult to injury when they trounced Oconto High, 100-0. East High scored 15 touchdowns: seven by Van Laanen, three each by Binish and Lambeau, and two by Wittig. Curly converted 10 goals after touchdown, giving him 28 points on the day. Several other players and officials were mentioned in the article. Sammy Cohn substituted for Harry Pelegrin at left guard, and George Dewey Theisin came in for Casey Loomis at right end. Other starters were Leonidas Edward Lee" Jonte at center, Nathan Nate" Abrams at left guard, and Irving Schmitz at right tackle. The final score was quite amazing, considering periods in those days were only 10 minutes long. Curly and his teammates scored a touchdown on an average of every 2 minutes and 40 seconds. Just imagine, if quarters in high school games back then had been 12 minutes long, then Curly's team would have scored 3 more TDs and 2 more PATs to make the final score, 120-0.

A few days later *The Press-Gazette* sportswriter printed a short story about the two high school football teams in the city. He wrote about how the two squads were becoming more adept at using the forward pass in their games. He cited Charlie Mathys from West High and Curly from East as being particularly gifted in heaving the spirals, and either boy is good for 30 yards or more." This is the first mention of Lambeau using the forward pass as a weapon and a strategy, a talent he would employ in the future to revolutionize pro football. Through three games East High scored 192 points and allowed a big fat goose egg to their opponents. The Hill boys, as they were called in the newspaper, lost their next game against Appleton, 16-6, but not because of Curly. Van Laanen, Theisen, Flatley, and he were cited as the only four East players who played real football" that day.

On the same page in the *Press-Gazette*, Curly got his picture in the paper along with a story about him and his participation in the loss to Appleton. The article was entirely positive and bordered on true adulation by the writer. His admirer started the story by referring to him as Curly instead of using his birth name. Could this have been the birth of the local idolization of Earl Louis Lambeau? The next day East High teacher Don Birdsall made true his promise to give a sweater to the first player to score a touchdown against the Papermakers. Since the only score of the game was by Lambeau, he received the prize. So, the answer to the previous question about Curly's popularity is a very resounding yes. In support of this claim, his surname appeared an incredible 20 times in the article reporting the very next game, which was against Marinette. Names of the other players were mentioned a total of 34 times. The Curly Lambeau legend had just begun.

Proof that Curly now stood atop the Green Bay sports popularity mountain came a few weeks later when East High squared off with West High. Curly was mentioned 27 times, while West High's star player Charlie Mathys appeared 21 times. Curly's running mate at left halfback Bill Wittig saw his name in print 19 times. Quarterback Frank Van Laanen had 10 mentions. Tackle and captain Frank Flatley saw his name in the article only four times. Earl Louis Lambeau had become the star on the city's football Christmas tree at age 16. He would remain there for 50 years in life and even more in death.

♦♦♦

Track and field proved to be another sport Lambeau could prove his athletic skills. As a sophomore in the spring of 1915, he ran in several events and exercised his muscles in the field as well. In the meets where the East High lads participated, Curly finished in the money in nearly every competition he entered from the 220-yard dash to the hammer throw. He proved himself to be an all-around athlete with skills that would stay with him into his 30s.

Unfortunately, Curly broke a leg in the middle of September that fall, forcing him to miss most of the football season. He finally got into a game on November 13 against Appleton, playing a few downs for Pete Abrohams at tackle. That position didn't require him to run very far or very fast. He played a little more in the annual East High versus West High fracas on Thanksgiving Day, substituting for Frank Jenske at quarterback.

The following spring Curly was elected captain of East High's track and field team. Once again, he showed his athleticism in the 220 dash, discus, shotput, hammer throw, and relay team. In their first meet that spring, a competition of 15 schools that was held at Ripon High School, the East High team finished in a tie for 12th place, scoring one point. Of course, Curly garnered that single mark for his side by finishing third in the hammer throw.

Curly also played baseball that spring and summer on the city team in the Bay Valley League. He saw action as the Green Bay team's third baseman, left fielder, and right fielder. Although he was speedy on the gridiron, he was only average on the basepaths. With the bat, he was a leader on the team, usually hitting third or cleanup and raking multiple hits in most games. Considering Curly was only 18 years old, he played quite well bearing in mind most of his team, the Green Bay Moose, and their opponents consisted of men in their 20s.

Yes, you read it right! The team was sponsored by the Moose Lodge of Green Bay, which also sponsored a bowling league in the city. Just imagine if the Moose Lodge had sponsored the city's football team instead of the packing company that did. The Green Bay Moose? Just doesn't have the same ring as Packers, does it?

♦♦♦

Lambeau's baseball season came to a halt once East High's football practice started on September 6. The first order of business for new teacher and head football coach Ralph Canright was the election of the team's captain and play-caller in the huddle. Of course, the only nominee was the best athlete in the city: Earl Louis Lambeau.

Former West High assistant football coach William Harold Cully" Collette authored a September 7, 1916 *Press-Gazette* article about East High's first practice, and he had this to say about the big Belgian.

> ***"Captain 'Curly' Lambeau has entirely recovered from his broken ankle of last year and should be about the class of the backs in the state. It would be hard to imagine a man with more qualifications for the ideal football player than Lambeau possesses. He is bigger than ever and has lost none of his accuracy with the punt and forward pass."*** *(Author's italics)*

Collette was a man who knew the strategy of winning football in his day. He played halfback for four years at Beloit College and was elected team captain his senior year 1911. After graduating from Beloit, he attended the law school at the University of Michigan, while playing football for the Wolverines in 1912 and 1913. While at Michigan, he sometimes took the train to Detroit on Sundays to play with the Ann Arbor pro team against regional competition. He then moved to Green Bay where he took a teaching position at West High School. With his experience on the gridiron at Beloit and Michigan, West High football Coach Harold White asked him to join his staff for the 1914 campaign, and Cully accepted.

In the September 26, 1914 issue of the Green Bay *Press-Gazette*, a very interesting item presented further proof that the Packers were not founded by either Curly Lambeau or George Whitney Calhoun. It read:

> ***"Manager (Clarence) Dashnier of the City team announced last night that he had secured the services of Harold Collette at half back ..." (Author's italics)***

Later that year, Collette accepted an offer from a school in a suburb of Louisville, Kentucky where he would be teaching in a regular classroom and coaching both football and basketball. His time at the Tharp school ended when classes were let out for the summer. With no hesitation, Collette hastened back to Green Bay to be with his family. Once again, he was hired by West High to teach and coach. The difference this time around was he was made head coach of the football team.

Besides sports, Collette was very active in other activities. In October 1915, he was elected president of the Green Bay Choral Society. Collette had previously served as vice-president of the group.

Then other coaching opportunities were presented to Collette, starting with him taking the reins of a new team in the area. This bunch of footballers also had positions in the Supply Company of the Second Infantry of the Wisconsin National Guard unit located in Green Bay. News of the birth of this team appeared in the *Press-Gazette* on the 21st of September 1915. Several players' names appeared in the article, a few of whom would be found on future Green Bay city team rosters when they were known as the Packers.

In March 1916, Collette left Green Bay and enrolled in the law school of the University of Wisconsin. He was soon initiated into the Phi Delta Phi fraternity for law students. Later that spring, he played on the Law School's baseball team. Although he was still a student in the fall, he was asked to join the coaching staff of the Badgers football team to teach the backs how to play their positions on both sides of the scrimmage line. He accepted and helped Wisconsin to a 6-2 season.

Collette's life took two new turns in 1917. President Woodrow Wilson had campaigned for re-election on the promise that he would keep the U.S. out of the war in Europe. A month after his second inauguration he went before Congress and asked for a declaration of war against Germany and its allies. Three months later Collette joined the Army as a second lieutenant. Four months after that, he proposed to his sweetheart Florence Margaret Kerr. On December 10, they were married at St. John's Catholic Church in Green Bay. From this time on, Collette changed his career choice from lawyer to officer in the army for the next 30 years.

Returning to the article he wrote about East High's football future, Collette's praise for Lambeau was sincere and honest. In no way did he exaggerate Curly's abilities as an athlete. Furthermore, he showed his own personal integrity in praising the Belgian kid from the east side of town. Although Lambeau's legend had started off two years earlier, Collette's tribute put the stamp of legitimacy on it. Curly was going places, and the sky was the limit.

♦♦♦

East High had lost the annual Thanksgiving Day contest with West High for seven consecutive seasons. The game was played on Turkey Day for bragging rights in Green Bay, if nothing else. In September 1916 at their first practice, Curly and his teammates set out to break that streak. Captain Lambeau took their first step in that direction by clobbering Shawano, 34-0, at home. The game was highlighted by Curly dashing 75 yards for a touchdown in the second quarter. This was a solid start for the Hilltoppers.

The Eastsiders planted a right hook on the chin of the Appleton Papermakers the following week. Curly and company returned home to Green Bay as the victors of a 32-0 shredding of the Fox Valley squad.

Sturgeon Bay High came to town the next week and took a bruising from the Hilltoppers, 40-0. A rugged squad from Marinette came to town the week after that and fought Lambeau's bunch to a 7-7 draw. East might have won the game, but Captain Lambeau was laid out" early in the game, hindering his play from that point forward.

A trip to Menominee, Michigan, a prominent port city across the Menominee River from Marinette, proved fruitless for East High as the game ended in a scoreless tie. The two most exciting moments in the contest nearly changed the outcome. When Curly attempted a dropkick goal from 40 yards that hit an upright and ricocheted onto the field, the crowd went wild over the try. Then one official called a penalty on the Green Bay eleven for tackling too hard." When Lambeau as captain of his team disputed the call, the referee threw another flag and declared the game a forfeit and Menominee the winner. Fortunately, for the boys from the bay city, the other official argued both calls in favor of East High and the game resumed. The writer for the *Press-Gazette* remarked that the other officiator was satisfactory to the Green Bay team," insinuating the referee was biased in favor of the home team.

Playing on a sore ankle, the same one he broke the previous year, Lambeau led his team to a scoreless tie against a bigger Oshkosh eleven on the latter's home field. The Lumberjacks' record was only soiled by a tie with Green Bay West the previous week. This tie hurt the chances of Oshkosh winning the state title, but it helped West's odds of capturing the crown.

Captain Curly Lambeau capped his high school football career with the biggest upset of the year when he and his East High crew held off the mighty West High eleven in a close encounter, 7-6, on Turkey Day in Green Bay. West scored first but missed the goal after the TD. Later in the initial period, East fought their way down to West's 6 as time expired for the quarter. West's defense stiffened for three plays of two yards by Bell, one yard by Peplinski, and one yard by Lambeau. It was now do-or-die for East. Fourth down and goal to go. Bell took the snap, handed off to Lambeau, and Curly busted through West's wall for the tying touchdown. Fans on both sides of the field held their collective breath as East lined up for the point after touchdown try. Curly took the snap and dropkicked the ball through the uprights for the final scoring in the game. West High had won this annual contest seven years in a row prior to this match. Now East High, behind its stalwart captain, broke that streak as they took home the title of Green Bay City Champion.

Lambeau's senior class picture was printed in the newspaper. The caption beneath it read:

> ***"By great ground-gaining, heavy booting and hectic defense, Capt. Curley (sic) Lambeau of East high easily proved himself to be the star of the game."***

In short, Curly had reached the pinnacle of high school football in Green Bay and the surrounding area, perhaps the entire state, like William Harold Cully" Collette had written before the season had even started.

This would not be the last praise for the prowess of the Belgian kid from Green Bay.

♦♦♦

Come spring of 1917, Curly's high school athletic career wound down with him as captain of the track and field team. On page 85, of the school yearbook, *The Aeroplane*, presented a photograph of the team and a list of their events. Curly participated in Shot, hammer, discus, broad jump. He also ran anchor in the half-mile relay. At the North East Wisconsin Inter-Scholastic meet in Appleton, Curly won first individual honors."

Unfortunately, the *Press-Gazette* stopped covering the two city high schools' sports programs immediately after the early April story about the East High track team.

♦♦♦

Curly turned 19 years old that spring of 1917. He graduated from high school and spent his summer working for his father and playing baseball on the city team. Fortunately for him and every other young man under the age of 21, he was not old enough to register for the military draft that was enacted May 18, 1917 and declared that all men of the ages 21 thru 30 had to sign up. After the U.S. Supreme Court confirmed the Constitutionality of the initial act, Congress amended it by changing the ages to 18 thru 45, making Curly eligible. He registered on September 8, 1918.

In the fall of 1917, Earl Louis Lambeau went south to Madison to sign up for college and play football for the Wisconsin Badgers. *The Wisconsin State Journal* of September 27 stated Lambeau and several other players were expected to arrive on campus that same day. He apparently made it because two days later on page 8 of the *Green Bay Press-Gazette* George Whitney Calhoun, the newspaper's sports editor, wrote in his column, *Cal's Comment*,

> ***"Curley (sic) Lambeau's entrance at Madison has been heralded with joy by the university papers as the majority of football critics consider the Green Bay boy one of the best***

gridiron prospects that has ever been turned out of a high school."

The newspaper Cal cited was *The Daily Cardinal*, which mentioned Curly as one of the 40-some newcomers out for the freshman team. Cal also made mention of the fact that Lambeau would be ineligible to play on the varsity squad due to the rule that barred freshman from competing with the big boys. This was the last mention of Curly in the *Press-Gazette* until his last name appeared in the newspaper on Monday October 15 when he was acknowledged as the referee in the East High game against Algoma. The story appeared on page 3 of the paper and not on the Sport World section on page 5. Could it be possible that Mr. Calhoun didn't want the whole city to know that Curly was back from Madison? The question now was simple. Why was he back? Could it be that he quit the freshman team because he didn't get to play in the annual Frosh-Varsity game? *The Daily Cardinal* listed all 18 freshman who played in the practice contest, and Lambeau was not among them. So, did he quit and return to Green Bay with his tail between his legs? Or was he dismissed from the team for some bad behavior? Maybe he was simply homesick. It had to be one of the three. No matter which one it was, Calhoun didn't reveal it to the public in the *Press-Gazette.* Instead, rumors floated around town that he quit the freshman team because he wasn't getting a fair shake from the coach and assistants. That's not possible because he never picked up his football gear. Nobody really knows why he returned home from Madison. It's this writer's opinion that he simply came to the conclusion that the University of Wisconsin wasn't for him.

Lambeau received another mention in the newspaper 10 days later on page 7 in a Society News item titled Surprise Gathering," in which one:

"Earl Lambeau gave several musical numbers during the evening."

Apparently, someone forgot to invite Cal to the party or tell him about the article before it went to press. History is full of such little clues to the truth.

♦♦♦

Curly was back in Green Bay. Now what? He officiated that one game in early October, but what about November? What did he do now that college was over for him for this school year? He got a job, and he played a little football, of course.

On November 11, the Green Bay City All-Stars squared off against the Marinette Badgers. Calhoun wrote,

> ***"Green Bay had its first touch of semi-pro football here yesterday afternoon ..."***

The local team was made up of players from the city's club league, which was why they were called the All-Stars.

> ***"Curley** (sic) **Lambeau got away with long runs ..." He scored 2 touchdowns and kicked 3 goals from touchdowns."***

Curly took a hard knock in the third quarter that forced him from the field for the remainder of the game. Tickets were sold, and the proceeds went to the Red Cross chapter in Green Bay and to pay the visiting team for its expenses.

Curly's younger brother Raymond" became the star of the East High football team now that Curly had graduated. The *Press-Gazette* gave him a lot of ink, although not so much as the paper had given Curly during his time at East. More popularly known as Rummy, the younger Lambeau did his share of carrying the ball for Hilltoppers. Sadly, many other authors and writers mistook Rummy's exploits on the gridiron to be those of older brother Curly.

♦♦♦

Little is known about Curly in 1918 until he registered for the draft on September 12. The one curiosity about this record is Curly listed his occupation as *foreman* for the *Indian Packing Company.* What makes this odd? Well, the story goes that Curly didn't start working for the Indian Packing Company until January 1919, which is why he didn't go back to Notre Dame in the fall of 1919. Allegedly, Curly came home for Christmas in 1918 with a bad case of tonsilitis. Once he got over the ailment it was too late to go back to South Bend, so he took a job at the Indian Packing Company as a *foreman* on the loading dock. Now isn't that strange that he was made a foreman as soon as he was hired and he was only 19?

Let's back up to December 29, 1916. That's the day George B. Gifford, secretary-treasurer of the Indian Packing Company out of Providence, Rhode Island, arrived in Green Bay to take charge of the installation of machinery in the plant being erected in connection with the Green Bay Packing Company. He brought his family with him and planned on establishing a permanent residence in the city.

The initial goal of the two companies was to work together canning meat to be sold in grocery stores all across the Midwest, South, and West. Construction of the two packing plants began with a ground-breaking ceremony on June 3, 1916. The railroad yards for receiving animals for slaughter and for shipping the finished products once the two buildings were built and in full operation began early in March 1917. The final touch came that summer with the fencing of stockyards on the grounds. Hiring workers for the twin concerns began in October that same year when the packing plants finally became operational.

Did Curly get a job at the Indian Packing Company that very month? It's more than probable that he did because he was back in the city at that time, having quit the University of Wisconsin freshman team and having his name in the *Press-Gazette* in a society article. Was he made a dock foreman right away? It's possible because of two factors.

The first was his father. As previously mentioned, Marcel Lambeau was a very important individual in Green Bay and the surrounding environs. Just imagine 19-year-old Curly standing in line to get a job. More than likely, he was hired right away and given a post on the loading dock because one look at him said this strapping young fellow was absolutely fit for the job of dock hand. Also, he was a really likeable guy, so much so, that he stood out in a crowd. So said by his first wife Marguerite in a telephone interview conducted by this author.

Then there was the second factor. That was Curly himself. He was a natural born leader. Everyone who knew him recognized that in him. Star player on the gridiron, track and field champion, outstanding baseball player, captain of the team in all three sports.

Everyone in school looked up to him. Running a loading dock was right up his alley. Being the foreman was the equivalent of being the head coach.

So, yes. Being handed the job of loading dock foreman right off the bat is very believable. After all, he was Curly Lambeau, stud athlete and oldest son of the most powerful man in the area.

♦♦♦

The other important factoid about Curly was the single game he played for the city team, mostly known as the Green Bay Skidoos and in the papers as the Bays. Lambeau was a big hero in that scrap, along with Art Schmaehle who was the player-coach of the team and who would figure prominently in Curly's future. The game was played on Sunday September 15, 1918.

On the very next day, Curly boarded a train for South Bend, Indiana to play football. Why Notre Dame? Because Notre Dame is a Catholic college but more importantly, the Fighting Irish had a new head coach. His name was Knute Rockne who was already famous for developing the forward pass with Gus Dorais as a major weapon.

In 1913, Rockne and Dorais made college football history. Their names were plastered all over the sports sections of newspapers all across the country when they were selected for first teams of various All-American rosters, including that of Walter Camp. Rockne and Dorais utilized the forward pass as a major weapon to defeat a powerful Army team, 35-13. Their success revolutionized the game of football in the United States and Canada. This was Curly Lambeau's kind of football.

Professional football in the second decade of the 20th Century was just becoming a popular sport, especially in the Midwest. While still working as an assistant coach at Notre Dame, Rockne played pro ball for the Akron Indians in 1914. The following season he and Gus Dorais, his best friend and teammate at Notre Dame, signed on with the Massillon Tigers, where they led their team to the title of the Ohio State League. After two more years playing with the pros, Rockne took over as head coach and athletic director at Notre Dame in February 1918.

Curly Lambeau read about Rockne becoming the head coach at Notre Dame in *Cal's Comment* in the *Press-Gazette.* Rockne heard about Curly from a student at Notre Dame named Archie Duncan, a former opponent of Lambeau's who played quarterback at Green Bay West High in 1915. Rockne needed a fullback, so he wrote to Lambeau and asked him to come to Notre Dame. Curly accepted the honor. His name was listed with three more young Green Bay students on page 4 of the September 23, 1918 newspaper.

When coach and player met in South Bend, neither man was disappointed in the other. Curly could run as fast as anyone else on the team. He could block, tackle, pass the ball, and catch it when it was thrown to him. The only player on the team better than Curly was the immortal George Gipp.

Lambeau scored the first touchdown of the 1918 season for Notre Dame against Case Western, a school located in Cleveland, Ohio. Curly's name appeared in the papers sporadically for the remainder of the football season. Then he fought in a club" boxing match in December after the gridiron schedule had finished. The bout lasted a mere 26 seconds before Lambeau's opponent suffered an ankle injury and had to throw in the towel, making Curly the winner by default. The kid from Green Bay probably would have won anyway; he was that tough.

The following summer Curly received his final mention in the South Bend *Tribune* on August 9. A list of the previous season's players appeared on page 10. All of those guys would be returning with the exceptions of *Larson, center and Lambeau, halfback, will not be eligible."* Gee, not eligible? That can only mean one thing. Larson and Lambeau had flunked out of school at the end of the first semester. Does that mean the story about him coming home for Christmas with a bad case of tonsillitis was true and he took a job at the packing company are fictional? He could have been ill, but he already had the position at the cannery. The tale about Curly coming home because he was ill was another fairytale cooked up by Lambeau's number one promoter George Whitney Calhoun. It wouldn't be the last such fable Cal would concoct about Curly.

Getting the boot from Notre Dame turned out not to be a bad thing for Curly. Actually, it turned out to be a lucky break for him. He could go back to work at the Indian Packing Company and play baseball for the company team in the spring and summer. Then in the fall he could play football on the city" team. Best of all, he could propose to his high school sweetheart Marguerite Van Kessel and get married that summer. No more college classes for him. To Curly, his dreams were coming true. Who knew? Maybe some baseball scout might see him play and offer him a spot on one of the professional teams in Wisconsin. Or just maybe he could hook up with one of the many rising professional football teams around the Midwest.

However, Curly's number one priority was marrying the girl he loved more than sports. Her name was Marguerite Marie Van Kessel. She was born April 30, 1899 in Green Bay. Her parents were John and Julia Vilim Van Kessel. Marguerite was the first of four daughters. Her parents immigrated to America from Europe; her father from Holland and her mother from Prague, the capital of the Bohemian Province of the Austro-Hungarian Empire.

This author had the privilege of interviewing Marguerite on two occasions. She revealed many facts about Curly. Some of them appearing initially in previous volumes of *The History of the Green Bay Packers* and now repeated in these pages in greater detail along with other undeniable facts of Curly's involvement with the Packers in their early days.

My favorite story Marguerite told me was how Curly would go out of his way every day to walk a few extra blocks from his house to hers just so they could take the same bus to work each morning. She said,

> ***"He would often throw a pebble or an acorn at my bedroom window to let me know he was waiting for me to come down and talk to him before the bus would come by."***

That little anecdote says a great deal about Curly as a person. He may have been a big-time jock to the fans in Green Bay, but to Marguerite he was truly a romantic because he stole her heart.

♦♦♦

The first attempt at someone writing the history of the Packers appeared in the pages of the *Green Bay Press-Gazette* in the late 1930s. During those years, the sports pages of the newspaper published a flashback column during football season retelling facts of Packer games on certain dates 5, 10, and 15 years earlier. Every once in a while, an article glorifying Lambeau in particular would appear, always on the first page of the sports section. On Wednesday, September 23, 1936, such an article appeared on page 21 titled:

Curly Lambeau Is Dean of Pro League Coaches

The story had no byline, so we can't be certain who wrote it. Probably a columnist for either the UPI or AP wire services. Curly isn't mentioned in the story until the third line of the third paragraph.

> ***"Curly Lambeau of the Green Bay Packers has been with the Wisconsin team ever since it entered the league in 1922, in fact was one of the organizers of the club several years before that."***

Obviously, the sportswriter who concocted this little gem had very little knowledge of the history of the Packers up to that date.

#1: The Packers entered the league" in 1921 when the Clair brothers, John and Emmett, were granted a franchise in the fledgling American Professional Football Players Association. Sad to say, their franchise was taken back after that first season when George Halas of the Chicago Staleys (Chicago Bears, starting in 1922) snitched on Curly for using a trio of college players from Notre Dame (whom Halas coveted for his newly christened franchise, the Chicago Bears) in the non-league game after the conclusion of the APFPA season. Lambeau arranged a contest with the Racine Legion because the Packers and Legion were the two best teams in Wisconsin and each club wanted the mythical state title. The game ended in a 3-all tie, leaving the claim on a state title divided between the two teams. Nobody thought the fracas was a big deal until the Milwaukee newspapers reported that Curly had used those three fellows from Notre Dame in the game. Of course, the Cream City press retracted the story a few days later after some urging" from their colleagues in

Green Bay. The powers-that-be at Notre Dame were—gee, how to put this—stark raving outraged over this misappropriation of their students' gridiron talents. Furthermore, the Notre Dame folks were enraged by another scandal involving nine other players on Rockne's team. Something had to be done. The end result was the Clairs forfeited their franchise. Curly tried to get it back, but Halas said no dice until August when he realized he needed the Packers as an opponent that season because the train ride to Green Bay was a tad shorter than it was to any of the eastern NFL teams. Curly was granted the franchise, and the Packers were back in business.

#2: The Packers weren't organized by Curly. Neither was he one of the organizers" of the earlier semi-pro incarnation of the Packers. The first Green Bay city team played in 1895 when the Green Bay Athletic association and the West Side Athletic association combined to make the city team. So stated the *Press-Gazette* on page 5 September 9, 1895. The team played its first game on October 19, 1895 against the Stevens Point Normal School. The college boys drubbed the Bays, 48-0.

Green Bay had a city team off and on for the next 25 years whenever some fellow with leadership qualities put a team together and scheduled contests with other city teams in Northeast Wisconsin and the Upper Peninsula of Michigan.

#3: As previously stated, Lambeau played in the city team's first game of the 1918 season before departing for Notre Dame. He didn't start that team either. He didn't start the 1917 team, although he played in the lone game it played that year. Both of those teams were organized by Curly's high school buddy Nate Abrams.

#4: The first fairytale about Lambeau said he came home from South Bend at Christmas time 1918 because he had tonsillitis or the flu, depending on which story one heard. He was expelled from the school for poor grades.

#5: The second fairytale said Lambeau and newspaperman George Whitney Calhoun ran into each other in downtown Green Bay a few days before he was to get married. Cal allegedly coaxed Curly into staying in Green Bay and playing for the city team instead of going back to South Bend and blocking for George Gipp for another season. The problem with that tale is simple. Students at Notre Dame were not permitted to marry until after they graduated. That was the rule back then, and it was still the rule the last time this author checked. Therefore, Mr. Lambeau already had plans to stay in Green Bay and settle down with the girl of his dreams.

#6: On August 14, 1919, a meeting of men interested in playing on the city team that year was held in the offices of the *Green Bay Press-Gazette*. Lambeau was there, of course, and he was elected to be captain of the team. Most likely unanimously. After all, he was the local sports hero and he had played at Notre Dame. However, he was not elected to be coach. That job went to Big Bill" Ryan, who had coached West High in 1916 and 1917 and a service eleven in 1918. Ryan also coached West High in 1919. The most important historical fact in this article was this sentence:

> ***"G. W. Calhoun will again manage the eleven this season." (author's italics)***

This can only mean one thing: Green Bay had a city team the previous year.

#7: At the same time that Calhoun was calling for players to meet at the newspaper's offices, the articles made it clear that the Indian Packing Corporation would be sponsoring the football team just like it had sponsored the city's baseball team, which was also called the Packers by the newspapers. There was no mention anywhere that Curly Lambeau talked the corporation's management into putting up the money for jerseys. However, there was this sentence:

> ***"The uniforms, which are being furnished by the Indian Packing Corporation, will be here in time for the opening game and the Packers" will be outfitted in the college style." (author's italics)***

Possibly, Lambeau *could have asked* his bosses to pony up the dough for the jerseys, but there was no mention of it in the newspapers until two decades later when all *the tall tales* about Curly hit the fan.

In summation, Earl Louis Curly" Lambeau did not *found* the Green Bay Packers. However, as the local sports hero and all-around nice guy that he was back then, Curly was the absolute impetus behind the formation of the Green Bay Packers football team, even though it took four years to get the organization on firm footing. (That story can be read in the first book in this series of the most incredible pro sports team in history.)

♦♦♦

Curly Lambeau did convince his employers to purchase a franchise in the American Professional Football Association (APFA) in 1921. He wanted to get the Packers into the new league in 1920 when owners and managers of 14 teams from New York, Ohio, Michigan, Indiana, and Illinois met in Ralph Hay's Hupmobile showroom September 17, 1920 in Canton, Ohio, but neither Curly nor Cal heard about the confab in time to take part in it.

Just as he had been in 1919 and 1920, Lambeau was captain of the 1921 Packers and one of its star players, but he was not the coach. Joe Hoeffel was the coach. The only coaching Curly did that year was at East High School. Neither did he represent Green Bay at the APFA meeting in Chicago on August 27, 1921. Emmett Clair had that honor and responsibility.

After he lost the franchise for the Clair brothers, Lambeau tried to get it for himself. Much to his chagrin, the newly renamed pro league turned him down—initially. His application for a spot in the newly named National Football League was held in limbo until the summer meeting in August when he was finally granted a place in the toddling NFL. All he had to do was post a $1,000 bond. He forked over the dough that came primarily from his old friend Nate Abrams. Lambeau mailed a certified check to league secretary Carl Storck, and the actual document was presented to Earl L. Lambeau at the summer meeting August 19, 1922. Upon returning to Green Bay, Lambeau handed the certificate of membership in the NFL to Nate as collateral for loaning him the bucks to get the franchise. Curly had already named himself head coach, captain, and general manager, just like George Halas did when he received the franchise for his Chicago Bears.

From that event until the executive committee forced him to resign from his posts with the Packers, Earl L. Curly" Lambeau built a true legend for himself. He brought the forward pass into the league as a major weapon that made the Packers a team not to be taken lightly. Better than that, Curly recognized real talent when he saw it. He had already enlisted the services of Howard Pierce Cub" Buck and Arthur Art" Schmaehl to bolster his team for the 1921 season. The next year Curly added Francis Louis Jug" Earp, another hefty lineman to go along with Buck. He convinced Charlie Mathys to leave the Hammond Pros and use his talents for the Packers. Former teammate at Notre Dame, Romanus Frank Nadolney, accepted an invitation to join the Packers for the 1922 campaign. In 1923, Lambeau added running back Myrton Nathan Myrt" Basing, a bull of a man and a graduate from Lawrence College in nearby Appleton, Wisconsin. (Basing can also be found on the author's wife's family tree.)

With three consecutive winning seasons on his coaching resumé, Curly's talent as a recruiter began to take shape. He did have help from the city's business community. Verne Clark Lewellen left his home state of Nebraska to play for the Packers, starting in 1924, and he practiced law in a local firm. Several other players found off-season employment in Green Bay and its satellite cities. In 1926, Ivan Wells Tiny" Cahoon, a native of Baraboo, Wisconsin and a graduate of Baraboo High, came home from far off Gonzaga University in Spokane, Washington to play for the Packers. When the Milwaukee Badgers folded after the 1926 season, Curly signed Lavvie Dilweg who was also hired by a local law firm. Then he convinced another graduate from Marquette University, Joseph Aloysius Red" Dunn, to leave the Chicago Cardinals and call signals for the Packers. In 1928, he added Bo Molenda from the New York Yankees when it became apparent that team was on the verge of folding. Earlier that year, Curly talked to All-American end Thomas Acton Tom" Nash from the University of Georgia into coming north and playing for the Packers.

Lambeau's best year for recruiting came in 1929. He added a trio of superstars: Johnny Blood, Cal Hubbard, and Mike Michalske. Curly realized he needed more talent on defense. Hubbard stood 6-

2 and weighed 253 pounds. Michalske tipped the scale at 210, and he measured six feet tall. Both men were all muscle and quickness. Blood was an all-purpose back. He could catch passes on both sides of the scrimmage line, run like the wind, and throw the ball as well as any QB in the league. Along with Dunn, Molenda, Nash, Dilweg, Cahoon, and Lewellen, the Packers captured the NFL title three straight years, the only team to do so until the Packers repeated that feat under Lombardi three decades later.

Earl Louis Lambeau's legend was made by that feat. Curly won three more NFL crowns in 1936, 1939, and 1944. He directed the Packers to 15 consecutive winning seasons from 1933 thru 1947. Over his tenure leading Green Bay, Curly's boys had only three losing seasons. He and dozens of his players can be found in the Pro Football Hall of Fame. The only coach who can match Lambeau in the annuls of the NFL during the pre-merger era would be his archrival and close friend George Papa Bear" Halas who also won six titles.

After being forced to resign after the 1949 season,* Lambeau was hired by the Chicago Cardinals. Under Hall of Fame Coach Jimmy Conzelman, the Cardinals had won the NFL title in 1947, then lost the title game the following year. After Conzelman resigned to focus on his off-season job in early 1949, the owner, Mrs. Violet Bidwill hired Phil Handler and Buddy Parker as co-head coaches for the Redbirds. Under that system, the Cards slipped to 2-4 and Handler was fired. Parker then directed the team to a 4-1-1 finish for an overall record of 6-5-1. When Curly became available, Violet fired Parker and signed the unemployed coach.

Lambeau entered his time with the Cardinals determined to show the powers-that-be in Green Bay were totally wrong to send him packing. Unfortunately for Curly, his fire to win didn't transfer to his players. The Cardinals were creamed by the Eagles 45-7, in the season opener. Curly gave his players a good verbal thrashing for the beating they had taken, and they responded by smashing their next opponent, 55-13. Of course, the team they squashed was the Baltimore Colts, a new eleven in the NFL, thanks to the merger between the leagues. The Colts won only one game that year. Who did Baltimore beat? Why, the Packers, of course, 41-21. Curly had a little chuckle when he heard that score.

Losing to the Bears and then to the Cleveland Browns ruined Lambeau's mood until his boys took down Washington on the road and New York at home to give the Cardinals a 3-3 record at the halfway point in the season. His Redbirds lost their first two battles of the second half, 10-7 in a close encounter with the Browns and then a 51-21 spanking by the Giants in Yankee Stadium. Curly got a good measure of revenge on the Eagles in Philadelphia, 14-10. Now 4-5 on the season, the Cardinals faced the 4-5 Steelers at Comiskey Park and lost, 28-17. The next week the Bears came to the Southside, and Curly's eleven got even with Halas's squad, 20-10. One game to go in his initial campaign in Chicago, Lambeau felt certain his team would give him one more win and 6-6 season. Sadly, for him, the Steelers were at home, and they hammered the Cardinals, 28-7, scoring on three long pass plays and one really long gallop from scrimmage.

Lambeau's time with the Cardinals ended after 10 games the next year. His Cards managed to beat the Bears in Comiskey Park in the second game of the season. Then the Southsiders lost five in a row before squeaking by the San Francisco 49ers in Frisco, 27-21. With two more losses on the books, Curly announced his resignation, effective
February 1, 1952. He stated in the *Chicago Tribune*,

> ***"I regret leaving Chicago where the Cardinals fans have supported us loyally and I am especially sorry to part company with the players, who have given me all the co-operation any coach could ask. However, I don't fit into the Cardinal organization."***

The Chicago newspapers tried to tell both sides of the story, but they failed miserably. Arch Ward's story favored Lambeau, while Harry Warren presented the Cardinals' management's point of view. A comparison of the two articles gave readers a choice of which side to believe: Coach Lambeau or Managing Director Walter Wolfner who just happened to be married to the team's owner, the widow of the late Charles W. Bidwill, Sr.

Ward quoted Curly:

> *"I regret leaving Chicago where Cardinal fans have supported us loyally and I am especially sorry to part company with the players, who have given me all the co-operation any coach could ask. However, I don't fit into Cardinal organization. I'm going to try with every ounce of energy I possess to whip the Washington Redskins in Comiskey Park Sunday and the Bears in Wrigley Field a week from Sunday. I know every member of the squad shares my determination. I'll continue to fulfill my obligations to the club to the best of my ability until my contract expires or until I am relieved of command. I am working on the draft list as diligently right now as if I intended to remain with the Cardinals indefinitely."*

Warren quoted Wolfner:

> *"Curly Lambeau will remain as head coach of the Cardinals for Sunday's game with the Washington Redskins and with the Bears a week later in Wrigley Field." He added: In his announcement in The Tribune, Mr. Lambeau expressed a desire to whip the Redskins and the Bears in the two remaining games of the season. In support of our contention that we have never interfered with Mr. Lambeau at any time, we see no reason to take action until*

after the season is over. We have told Mr. Lambeau repeatedly that he was in charge of the team, and we would stand back of any decisions he made."

Wolfner continued his statement by mentioning dissension in the coaching staff and hinted that Curly was at the center of it. He went on to reveal some incidents concerning the assistant coaches, but he didn't point any fingers at anyone in particular.

That very evening Wolfner showed his true colors by telling Lambeau that his services were no longer needed and that he shouldn't bother to show up for the game against the Redskins. Curly shot back that he would be in the stadium even if he had to buy a ticket to do so. At the same time, Wolfner handed the coaching reins to assistant coaches Phil Handler and Cecil Isbell for the last two games of the campaign. Under their tutelage, the Cardinals lost to Washington on a last-minute field goal, then stuck it to their crosstown rivals the following week, downing the distressed Bears, 24-14, by utilizing a new formation that they had implored Lambeau to use earlier in the season, to which he said no.

Harry Warren took more shots at Curly for being out of touch with the many new innovations in the pro game. Arch Ward continued to give his support to Lambeau, writing how Curly's six NFL titles and 25 winning seasons in Green Bay proved he was a very dynamic man on the sidelines.

Wolfner continued to meddle with the Cardinals players and coaches throughout the rest of his time in the front office. The result? A parade of losing seasons and a long list of disenchanted players and coaches.

In reality, Earl Louis Lambeau and his players pulled off some miraculous wins in his short time on Chicago's Southside in spite of the constant interference they received from the Buddha-shaped boss of the Cardinals Walter Wolfner.

♦♦♦

The following year George Preston Marshall, the very volatile owner of the Washington Redskins, went on a rant aimed at his more than capable head coach Dick Todd after the 49ers clubbed the Redskins,

35-0, in a pre-season game in San Francisco. Marshall took the beating as if it had been a regular season contest that actually meant something. Marshall's complaint against Todd was unleashed because the coach used mostly rookies and backups and only a few of his regulars in the game. As a result, Todd resigned his post just before Washington's next pre-season contest against the Rams in Los Angeles. Todd cited his need to attend to his ranch and cattle business back in Texas as his reason for stepping down. The reality was simple. Todd had his fill of Marshall and his meddling with the team.

The first name mentioned to replace Todd was the legendary former coach of the Green Bay Packers Earl Louis Lambeau. Curly immediately stated he had not been contacted by Marshall to fill the open position. The next day the Skins' owner presented a list of four candidates to become the next head coach in Washington. First on the list was Lambeau, followed by Red Strader, Greasy Neale, and Hunk Anderson. Note that all four men had nicknames that separated them from the hoard of other football coaches. Of this group, Curly had the most experience as a winning head coach in the NFL. Marshall offered him the job in a telephone call, and Lambeau accepted with only one stipulation. He told Marshall he would coach the Redskins for the next two years. After that? They could cross that bridge when they reached it. A half hour later backfield coach Jerry Neri turned in his resignation and the greatest quarterback of his time Sammy Baugh was named to replace Neri as a player-coach.

Lambeau took charge of the Redskins the next day. He wasted no time making changes to the offense and defense. Within a week, he realized he had made a few mistakes and made more changes. He kept working as hard as he ever had in Green Bay. The results over the last three pre-season games were not good. All losses, including one to the Packers at Blues Stadium in Kansas City, 13-7.

The 1952 NFL regular season campaign opened on a positive note for Lambeau and his Redskins. They met the Chicago Cardinals in Comiskey Park on a Monday night game. Washington handed the Cards a 23-7 defeat, and there was joy in the Nation's Capitol. It didn't last. The following Sunday the Redskins traveled to Milwaukee to face the Packers in Marquette Stadium. Road-weary from traveling from Los Angeles to San Antonio to Kansas City to Norman, Oklahoma and then to Chicago, the Redskins finally ran out of gas and played like it against a mediocre Green Bay eleven, losing 35-20.

After losing the next week to the Cardinals at home, 17-6, the Redskins traveled to Pittsburgh and came away with a narrow 28-24 victory. The future looked bright, but it turned out to be one black cloud after another, losing six straight games, four of them by a TD or less. Washington's season ended on a really positive note, dumping the Giants in New York and clipping the Eagles wings in the season finale.

Curly's second season at the helm of the Redskins began on a positive note again with a 24-13 victory over the hapless Cardinals in Comiskey Park. That game was followed up by a sister-kissing 21-all tie with the Eagles in Connie Mack Stadium in Philadelphia. The Giants came to Washington for a week three clash, and Curly's boys came away with a 13-9 win.

With a 2-0-1 record, the Redskins looked like a real challenger for the conference title. Then the Browns came to town. Not good. Cleveland smacked the Skins, 30-14.

A short trip to Baltimore the next week resulted in another defeat, 27-17. Another road game, this one in Cleveland, resulted in a 27-3 blowout by Paul Brown's club. Although bruised and battered, Curly's team hitched up their pants and played their best game of the year, dumping the Cards, 28-17, in Griffith Stadium.

Papa Bear's Monsters of the Midway came to town the following week, and the Redskins gave them everything they had for three quarters, holding the lead at 24-20. Then the Bears mounted a final charge with George Blanda completing a short pass to Eddie Macon who carried the ball into the end zone for Chicago's winning score, 27-24.

Furious that his team ran out of gas in the fourth quarter of the Chicago game, Curly worked his players much harder the next week. The result? Redskins 24, Giants 21. More hard work followed, and Curly's boys hung a loss on Pittsburgh, 17-9, in the Steel City. In the 11th week of the season, the Eagles came to town, and the Redskins shut them down, 10-0.

A victory over Pittsburgh in the final game of the season meant a second-place finish for the Redskins and a $400-bonus for each Washington player. The win appeared to be in the bag at the end of three periods as the home team led, 13-0. Then the defense gave up one touchdown and an extra point to Pittsburgh, and the offense did the same when QB Eddie LeBaron threw an interception that resulted in a five-yard sprint to paydirt by the thief. A PAT followed, giving the Steelers a 14-13 triumph and leaving Washington with a 6-5-1 record for 1953.

Lambeau went into the draft in January with a bona fide plan of attack to bolster his roster enough to put the Redskins in the middle of the fight for the Eastern Conference title. He convinced all of his picks to come to Washington instead of skipping off to the Canadian Football League. Training camp in California jumped off to a good start as his boys went to work right away, working hard to get to learn Curly's offense for the first preseason game, a tilt set against the Rams at the Coliseum in Los Angeles. Obviously in better shape than the visiting squad, the home team came out running and never slowed down, spanking the Redskins, 27-7. Coach Lambeau in Pittsburgh remarked after the game:

> ***"This was a team defeat. I haven't a good word to say for anyone and I'm not going to say what I could about what wasn't good."***

Over his entire career, Curly seldom placed blame on his players for losing a game.

Next up for the Skins were San Francisco's 49ers *just three days* later in Sacramento. Again, Curly's boys were thrashed, this time 30-7. But the outcome of the game wasn't the big story that night.

After the poor showing, Washington's volatile owner George Preston Marshall ran into three players entering their hotel room. One man was carrying a paper bag. Marshall asked what was in the sack. The fellow spoke the truth. Beer." Georgie exploded and took the brews away from them. The players then headed off to the lobby where they found Lambeau and told him what had happened. Curly then sought out Marshall. They argued. Marshall said the players were guilty of breaking training. Lambeau said he allowed *his* players to have a beer or two after a game. Marshall countered that alcoholic beverages were against the rules during training season. Curly responded that he made the rules for *his* players. Marshall retorted that *he* owned the team, so he made the rules. To make his point, he nudged Curly with a firm push to his shoulder. Lambeau pushed back. Marshall shoved him away. Curly did the same to the owner. The boss then made the final move. He fired Lambeau officially the next morning, thus ending the legendary Earl Louis Curly" Lambeau's very long and stellar career in professional football.

Curly did coach the College All-Stars for three seasons in the annual charity game in Chicago, beating the NFL champion Cleveland Browns in his first year and losing the next two contests. Thus, his long career playing and coaching football came to an end.

♦♦♦

Earl Louis Curly" Lambeau passed away on June 1, 1965, from a heart attack suffered while visiting friends in Sturgeon Bay, Wisconsin. The official story states he died while mowing grass in his friend's yard. Of course, rumors of all kinds about his death circulated around Green Bay, but gossip is what it is. His demise had witnesses, and those few people must have their reports accepted.

Other facts about Lambeau must also be accepted, starting with the claims about Curly's coaching career with the Packers. The newspapers of the time never stated he was the coach of the team in 1919, 1920, and 1921. They reported his post as captain. Not until 1922 was Curly the actual coach of the Green Bay Packers, although many so-called historians state the contrary either out of ignorance or because of the company line" that still goes on to this day.

A piece on page 6 of the September 6, 1932 *Press-Gazette* refutes the claim that Lambeau founded the Green Bay Packers. Oddly, this letter to the editor has never been marked for clipping like so many thousands of other newspaper articles about Lambeau and the Packers until this author did so on August 11, 2024.

This raises the question: Why didn't Packers historians previous to this series cite this letter to the editor in their books and articles? Could it be because this missive was proof that the legend that was built around local hero Curly Lambeau, starting in the late

1930s, was really just that, a fable, a tale devised to help the franchise raise more money for the team at a time when *The Great Depression* was still ravaging our nation?

The writer of this letter was Edmund D. Thiry, a railroad car inspector in Green Bay, born November 8, 1898 at a place called Thiry Dams in Red River Township, Kewaunee County, Wisconsin. Just like the man he admired so much, Edmund Thiry was also of Belgian heritage. He was also a big Packer fan all his adult life. Everyone around Green Bay knew him as Eddie. The news editor headlined Thiry's letter:

WANTS LAMBEAU DAY

Thiry's complete letter read:

> *Editor, Press-Gazette—Let's go Packers—Through your forum column may I suggest a procedure that occasionally occurs during baseball seasons? At these occasions a certain player or manager is being honored by the executive staff and the patrons for his courage, efficiency and sportsmanship he has shown during his service.*
>
> *Personally, I deem it is due time the people of this community have such a person to honor and respect in the parson (sic) of E.L. Lambeau manager of a thrice champion team, a feat that will be hard for mangers in years to come to equal.*
>
> *He as an individual deserves more credit for the honor than any since the Packer team originated. Truly the packing plant originated the team, (author's italics) but only the confidence the executives had who made*

a league entry in E.L. Lambeau prompted them to such action.

He in turn proved very capable by proving the honor they were seeking, a championship, a name for Green Bay. Personally, it would only seem fair that we extend this honor in favor of our team manager and have an E.L. Lambeau day the Sunday the Chicago Bears play here.

When you consider the confidence each individual player must have in him, for if they hadn't, he could not win championships. He is deserving a tribute he will never forget and considering what little effort if (sic) will mean on the part of patrons, and how much it will mean to the champion player manager.

I am not inclined to be selfish, but something seems to tell me he and his wonderful will ring the bell again this year for the fourth consecutive time.

Edmund Thiry
236 No. Broadway

Mr. Thiry resided in Green Bay from at least September 12, 1918, when he made out his World War I Draft Registration Card. He was living in Green Bay when Lambeau and the city team played their first game that fall and when the *Press-Gazette* reported Curly's departure for South Bend to play football for Knute Rockne at Notre Dame. Eddie worked at a lumber mill in Green Bay at that time. Then he found employment as a railroad car inspector a few years later and lived in Green Bay for the rest of his life, leaving this world June 23, 1986, at a local nursing home.

In short, Edmund D. Thiry and thousands of other Green Bay and Brown County residents were absolutely aware of the fact that Earl Louis Lambeau was *not* the founder of the Green Bay Packers in 1919 any more than he was the founder of the baseball team the packing company started that year. This is so because no one, especially not George Whitney Calhoun or Earl Louis Lambeau, contested Thiry's statement that the packing company founded the Packers.

Six years later, the very first mention of Lambeau being the founder of the Packers appeared in the *Press-Gazette.* The H.C. Prange Company published a full-page ad on page 5 of the September 10, 1938 edition that was actually more of an interview with Curly than it was an advertisement for the department store. This was the first time he was mentioned in the newspaper as being the founder of the Packers. The problem with this is none of the people in charge of advertising and management of the H.C. Prange Company in 1938 were living in Green Bay back in 1919. There's also the fact that the Green Bay city team had existed in one form or another since 1895.

Shortly after his death, the Greater Green Bay Labor Council unanimously adopted a resolution at their meeting on June 8, 1965. It called for the renaming of City Stadium in Curly's honor. Council President Clayton Smits sent a copy of the declaration to President Clarence Nier of the Green Bay Stadium Commission. It read:

> Whereas, Earl (Curly) Lambeau has contributed more to the recognition of Green Bay, nationally and even internationally, than any other native or adopted son of our city, and
>
> Whereas, the Green Bay Packer Football Club was *primarily his creation* (author's italics) and its growth and fame in earlier years largely due to his efforts and fighting spirit, and
>
> Whereas, the Lambeau" symbolizes the finest in professional football,
>
> Be it resolved, that the name of Green Bay City Stadium be changed to Lambeau Stadium" or Lambeau Field" in honor of Curly Lambeau.
>
> Be it further resolved that a copy of this resolution be delivered to the mayor and City Council of the City of Green Bay.
>
> Adopted unanimously this 8th day of June, 1965.
>
> Greater Green Bay Labor Council
>
> Clayton Smits, President.

Now why did the labor council suggest that the Packers were only *primarily* Curly's creation? This implies others were involved in the founding of the Packers, others most likely being George Whitney Calhoun and the Clair brothers. The council was overlooking the fact that Curly was granted a different franchise in the league in August of 1922. It can be said that this was when Curly founded the Packers, but the men who operated the team as a business needed a longer time than 17 years to declare an anniversary for the club. Thus, they made Curly the founding father in 1939.

♦♦♦

The following week the Green Bay City Council passed their own tribute to Lambeau. They praised Curly as a guiding light in the National Football League …" and earning accolades from sports fans throughout the world in his lifetime. In death he has become an integral part of Green Bay's history."

To show Lambeau's humble side, they presented an anecdote that contained his response to the first time the Green Bay Stadium Commission was requested to name City Stadium after him.

Boys, I am glad that you didn't take any action on naming the new stadium after me. I never played there, had no part in building it, and it is my opinion that the new stadium belongs to the people who built it, the citizens of Green Bay."

The council went on to say that Curly was not only the heart of Green Bay, but his heart was in Green Bay."

Then they ordered the clerk to spread this resolution upon the minutes of this meeting so that prosperity will be informed of our thoughts about an outstanding citizen."

The very next day *Press-Gazette* sportswriter Len Wagner wrote a scathing letter" to the City's Fathers. He railed about their so-called tribute of Lambeau that was allegedly the general feeling of the citizens of Green Bay. Wagner felt otherwise. So much so, that he sought a poll from the area's barber shops. He called 34 such establishments and asked the owners what his patrons were saying about the so-called tribute to Curly by the City Council. Much to his pleasure, he learned that the patrons of 23 shops agreed that the best tribute to be made for Lambeau was to name the stadium after him despite Curly's wish not to have his name put on the place. Four more indicated that they were somewhat in favor of the name change. Three barbers said their patrons were pretty much split even on the question. The last four said there wasn't enough discussion about the issue for them to establish an opinion one way or the other. Wagner closed off his letter" with a paragraph that made little sense.

> ***"Oh, and before I forget. If Mr. Lambeau was a humble man, as your resolution says, isn't it logical that he would protest having the stadium named after him? Isn't that what you would expect from a humble man? I do hope we have yet to hear about the 'proper' tribute."***

Apparently, Mr. Wagner didn't read his own words out loud. If he had, he may have realized that he was agreeing with the few fans who opposed the renaming of City Stadium.

At the July 6th meeting of the city council, the aldermen passed a resolution to honor Lambeau with a building named after him. That structure would be built on the stadium grounds. The vote was almost unanimous. Alderman Rhynie Dantinne was the only councilman to vote against the proposed memorial building.

At the July 20th meeting of the City Council, 21 aldermen voted to send "recommended" that City Stadium be renamed to honor Curly, but the council took no other action than sending the recommendation to the Stadium Commission. Mayer Donald Tilleman supported the council's suggestion to the commission.

On July 27, 1965, the special seven-man committee, named by city attorney and Stadium Commission president Clarence Nier, unanimously voted to rename City Stadium after Curly, calling it Lambeau Field. The committee members were Charles Brock, chairman, Arnold "Arnie" Herber, vice-chairman, and Andy Uram, all former Packers; Haydn Evans, WBAY, Ben Laird, WDUZ, John Torinus, Sr., Packers executive committee member (and a dear friend of this writer); and David A. Yuenger, *Press-Gazette.*

Finally, the Green Bay City Council voted unanimously at their Tuesday August 3, 1965 meeting to rename Green Bay City

Stadium after the legendary man who had done so much to make the Green Bay Packers an equally legendary organization, not just in professional football, but in all of professional sports around the world. Of course, the *Press-Gazette* writer embellished his version of Curly, calling him the founder and first coach of Packers. This would be true, if he was referring to the 1922 season when Lambeau was granted a franchise in the NFL and he named himself head coach as well as a player. But, as usual, the writer was referring to the 1919 town team as Curly's sole creation.

Earl Louis Curly" Lambeau founded the 1922 team and did everything he could to make the Packers survive *The Great Depression*, World War II, and the war between the NFL and AAFC. Yes, he had help from the businessmen of Green Bay and surrounding area, but they remained in the shadows while he remained the major focus of the Packers. He was truly a giant in the history of the National Football League for 33 years. Hardly anyone who knows his name does not immediately think of his native city. The people of Green Bay know in their heads and their hearts how much he meant to their city and their state.

Perhaps his headstone should read:

EARL LOUIS LAMBEAU
1898-1965

ALTHOUGH CURLY IS GONE HIS

L E G E N D

WILL LIVE ON FOREVER

Absolutely forever. Men like Curly aren't born every day in the world of sports. § § §

5

"Back to Work, Boys!"

General Manager Vincent Lombardi advised Coach Vince Lombardi that he'd better get his fanny in gear and push his players to the limit in 1965 because the schedule was not going to be a walk down Primrose Lane. Vince understood the boss completely. Two second place finishes in a row in the Western Division might be acceptable in some corners of the pro circuit, but they were totally unsatisfactory for a franchise that had risen to the top of the division three consecutive years with two of those seasons topped off with back-to-back NFL titles. Said the GM:

> ***"Either win that crown again, Coach, or maybe find another job."***

Heading into the 1965 training season, Lombardi faced the loss of three starting players. Ron Kramer was already gone, having played out his contract and wanting to play in Detroit to be close to his wife and children. Jerry Norton had decided to retire, and Dan Currie had been traded. To make matters worse, Jesse Whittenton was thinking about hanging up his cleats for good.

The loss of Kramer opened a spot for backup tight end Marv Fleming, a three-year veteran with strong hands. For Currie, Lombardi received Carroll Dale, a fleet pass catching flanker obtained from the Los Angeles Rams. Vince had picked up punter and place kicker Don Chandler from the New York Giants to replace Norton. Whittenton's possible departure and Norton's retirement left the defensive backfield with only five returnees: Willie Wood, Hank Gremminger, Herb Adderley, Tom Brown, and Doug Hart. If

Whittenton did retire, the first choice to replace him was Bob Jeter who was being moved to the defense. The next day Whittenton made his retirement official.

The linebacker corps would consist of veterans Ray Nitschke, Lee Roy Caffey, Dave Robinson, and Tommy Crutcher. Hot prospect Bill Curry from Georgia Tech was a major candidate to break into the defensive group.

♦♦♦

When camp opened July 21st, 70 veterans, draftees, and free agents reported for physicals at St. Norbert College. Those missing were three rookies who were at Northwestern University training for the College All-Star Game in Chicago. They were Bill Curry from Georgia Tech, Allen Brown from Ole Miss, and Junior Coffey from Washington. Not among the veteran players were Dan Currie, Jess Whittenton, Jerry Norton, and Ron Kramer.

Every man passed his physical, and the next day the rookies and veteran backs, ends, and centers would begin two-a-day drills at the Packer practice field at 10 o'clock that morning.

Lombardi let his assistant coaches and all his players know one very simple thing. They were there to win another championship. Anything less would be unacceptable. And he would work them every practice with that thought in mind. They had two weeks to get themselves in shape good enough to win the Bishop's Charities game with the Giants. A pre-season game or not, a loss would not suffice.

Much to his surprise, Lombardi was met with a crushing blow on the day the veterans were all due to report to training camp. Rugged Norm Masters, an eight-year stalwart at offensive tackle, reported to camp at St. Norbert College and handed the coach a surprise of the worst kind.

> ***"It's time to make the decision, and I felt it only fair to Coach Lombardi and the team to make the decision (to retire) before they made plans for the season."***

Acquired from the Detroit Lions in the 1957 Tobin Rote trade. Masters shared left tackle with Skoronski since 1959, except for the previous season when Skoronski was moved to center in wake of Jim Ringo's departure. Then he progressed to right tackle when guard Fuzzy Thurston was injured in mid-season.

Lombardi announced Masters' retirement, saying quite sadly,

> ***"Norm has been a great credit to the team. Not only for his football ability, but also for his lightness and jovial attitude. He is one of the great tackles in the league. Norm was smart enough to know that when a man feels he is not mentally ready to go, he deteriorates physically. Therefore, he felt that if he could not give 100 per cent, he should retire. Norm would not stay on unless he could do a great job."***

In this writer's opinion, Masters deserves to be in the Packers Hall of Fame. He played on three division winners and two NFL title winners for Lombardi. That is saying a lot for anybody.

Besides Masters' retirement, Lombardi released seven rookies, lowering the number of players in camp to 62.

With Masters retired, Lombardi considered Steve Wright, the rollicking 6-6 Kentuckian" and Lloyd Voss, the studious 6-4 transfer from the defensive platoon, as contestants for the tackle spot. Both men tipped the scale at 250 pounds, good weight for that time period. Also flashing some talent for the position were rookies Rich Koeper, 6-4, 245-pounder from Oregon State's 1965 Rose Bowl team, and Dick Herzing, 6-3 and 250-pounder from Drake University in Iowa. Voss and Wright were both in their second year with the Packers. When the season started, Wright won the job of offensive right tackle, and Voss was returned to defensive end backing up all-pros Willie Davis and Lionel Aldridge.

Unwelcome news struck the Packers on August 1. Lombardi lost his No. 1" draft choice indefinitely. Allen Brown, the 6-4½, 230-pound tight end from the University of Mississippi. Brown underwent surgery on his right shoulder at St. Vincent Hospital the next morning. There was no official estimate when Brown would be available to play. Best guess said he might not be ready until mid-season, if at all. Brown had actually been drafted in the third round behind Larry Elkins from Baylor and Grambling's Alphonse Dotson who were both lost to the AFL. Barring personnel switches, it also set the stage for a two-man struggle behind Marv Fleming, heir to the departed Ron Kramer. Jim Thibert from Toledo and the United Football League and Wofford's John Housel as the contestants. Brown's loss temporarily depleted the overall squad to 57.

The next day the celebrated "Ron Kramer Case" was finally resolved. But not, apparently, entirely to Lombardi's satisfaction.

Kramer had played out his option at the end of the previous campaign, then announced his desire to play for the Detroit Lions and only the team from the Motor City. He finally got his way when the Lions signed him to a one-year deal as a defensive end.

In return, Detroit surrendered their first-round draft pick in the next year's NFL draft as compensation to the Packers. This deal was brokered by Commissioner Pete Rozelle. Lombardi replied,

> ***"The decision of the commissioner that Ron Kramer be awarded to Detroit in return for a draft choice is under no circumstances to be understood to be a trade, but rather a decision by the commissioner."***

NFL rules at the time stipulated that when a player plays out his option and subsequently is signed by another team, his new team must compensate his old club with a player of comparable value.

Kramer finally got his wish, and Lombardi reluctantly got his.

On the next day, Lombardi trimmed the roster to 56. He cut rookie halfback Jim Chandler from the squad. This left 38 veterans and 18 freshmen in camp.

The Packers played their annual scrimmage game in the rain on Saturday night, August 7. The offense defeated the defense, 29-0. Placekicker Don Chandler showed off his talented toe by booting five field goals, the longest one sailing 48 yards early in the final quarter. Backup QB Zeke Bratkowski completed a 22-yard strike to Bob Long, and fellow backup Dennis Claridge hit ex-Ram receiver Carroll Dale for a 16-yard TD to finish off the scoring.

Watching the game from the press box, Lombardi was nothing but smiles afterward.

> ***"I thought we moved the ball well, considering the conditions. We didn't get it across the goal line too often, but we moved it well." When asked about the team's chances in the coming season, the coach played it cool, saying, That's hard to determine … when you're playing against yourself. It's almost double jeopardy."***

Behind the scene, Ol' Vince knew he had a solid team again. How solid? Time would tell.

§ § §

6

Pre-Season 1965

General Manager Lombardi started pre-season Game Week 1 by releasing two rookies. Offensive guard Joe (Buddy) Eilers of Texas A&M and defensive tackle Charles Harris out of Tennessee A&I were both placed on waivers. Neither man ever played in the NFL. This reduced the rookie roster to 16 men.

Joining the Packers' regular practice that Monday were College All-Stars Bill Curry, a center and linebacker from Georgia Tech, and Junior Coffey, a halfback from Washington. Curry had acted as long snapper for field goals and extra points in the scrimmage game, while Coffey filled in on special teams. Both men were expected to do more in the upcoming annual Bishop's Charities game against the revamped New York Giants at newly christened Lambeau Field.

At the third annual Meet the Packers" luncheon, Lombardi declared to more than 250 fans,

> ***"This is by far the best camp I've ever had since I have been with the Packers. There is more spirit, more determination, more of everything than I have seen since I have been with the Packers. If that same spirit and determination prevails, and it must, of course, there is no reason why we shouldn't have a very excellent team."***

Terming his 1965 squad: ***"by far the best conditioned football team I've ever had," Lombardi observed, "there are other things, however, and one of the most important is pride. So far, there is every indication that they have great pride. Pride, of course, must be constant—it is not something you can turn on and off like a light bulb. You must have it on Monday, Tuesday, Wednesday, Thursday, Friday, and Saturday, as well as on Sunday."***

A record crowd of 50,837 piled into Lambeau Field to watch the Packers hammer the New York Giants, 44-7. The Packer offense racked up 379 yards in total; 163 on the ground and 216 through the air. Green Bay stuffed the New York defense for six touchdowns. Bart Starr to Carroll Dale for 51 yards and Bob Long for eight yards. Ron Heller rushed for score number three, a one-yard smash behind second year tackle Steve Wright. Paul Hornung put up six with a two-yard burst to paydirt. Junior Coffey made his mark with a one-yard crash into the end zone. The biggest score of the night came from Tom Brown when he returned a punt 91 yards for the Pack's final TD. Don Chandler converted on five PATs and one field goal of 36 yards.

Come Monday after the pre-season opener, general manager Lombardi had to decide on who to cut to reduce the roster to 50 men. Placed on waivers were Ron Heller from Southern California, and defensive tackles Roger Jacobazzi from Wisconsin and Dick Herzing from Drake. This left the roster with 38 veterans and 12 rookies. This left only three rookie offensive backs to challenge the veterans. They were Bill Symons from Colorado, Junior Coffey from Washington, and Allen Jacobs from Utah. The Packers were only three players over the first cutdown deadline on August 31.

Next up for the Packers were the Monsters of the Midway, the Chicago Bears, at County Stadium in Milwaukee. For Lombardi, this was the first of three Bears weeks. Although the contest was nothing more than a meaningless pre-season game, he had every intent on handing the Windy City 11 their first loss of the year.

The big news of the week? Henceforth, the Packers would be dressing and disrobing in their commodious Lambeau Field quarters to strains of music from a stereo phonograph bought and paid for by the players. Bob Skoronski said,

> ***"We proposed it to Coach Lombardi, and he thought it was a good idea. The idea is to give the boys a little relaxation. We spend a lot of time out here."***

Equipment manager Dad Braisher added zest to the occasion by donning a ghoulish rubber mask and rendering a spirited solo on the pogo-cello", a wondrous contraption fashioned from a pole, piano wire, a covered cake tin with BB shot, a horn and cymbals, and played with notched bow". Braisher promised to perform only on special occasions, such as a home win.

A few days later GM Lombardi made one of his classic deals, this one with the Washington Redskins. Vince bought some insurance for Marv Fleming, his great tight end blocker and pass receiver. He bought the contract of Bill Anderson who had sat out one season to serve as an assistant coach at his alma mater, the University of Tennessee.

Rookie tight end Jim Thibert was the present backup for Marv, and he was doing good job. Even so, Vince's purchase of Anderson's services had a meaning. Fleming had the starter's job all lined up for the present; no replacing him, so then what?

Although Thibert had seen some action with the Edmonton Eskimos for one season in the Canadian League, Anderson's time in Washington had been close to phenomenal. After being drafted by Philadelphia Eagles in 1957, he was sold to Washington a few weeks later. In six seasons with the Redskins, big Bill caught 178 passes for an average of 17.1 yards per game. He was Washington's Rookie of the Year in 1958 and then their Player of the Year the following season. In 1961, he set a record by spearing 10 passes for 168 yards on November 19 against the Dallas Cowboys in the Cotton Bowl. He was elected to the Eastern Conference all-star team in 1960 and 1961.

On the same day that Anderson became a Packer, the

Packers were predicted by *Look Magazine* to defeat the Cleveland Browns for the National Football League championship that season. The magazine noted how the Packers had a fierce running game and quarterback Bart Starr who calls plays impeccably. Whereas the Browns, the team to beat in the East, most nearly matches the Packers in overall strength. Cleveland's only weakness seemed to be a shortage in the defensive reserves.

In the same article, the forecasted AFL champ from the previous year, the Buffalo Bills, would repeat as league champions by dumping the Kansas City Chiefs. KC was said to have a well-rounded crew who would break the San Diego Chargers' hold on the Western Division title.

Time would tell who would grab the two division crowns in each league and which of those teams would become their league's champs for 1965.

The Bears were coming to Milwaukee with a much-changed outfit than they had been the previous season. Chicago's roster had a lot of new faces; two in particular, first-round picks in the Draft, Dick Butkus, All-American middle linebacker, and Gale Sayers, the shiftiest running back in the country who tripled as a kickoff receiver and punt returner. The Bears had been off their feed in 1964 due to the loss of popular running back Willie Galimore and receiver John Farrington who were killed in a car crash just a few miles from the Bears training camp in Rensselaer, Indiana. A terrific draft for the 1965 draft and the signing of a few free agents to go along with some key trades were giving hopes in Chicago of at least a winning season in 1965. Bear fans' hopes that the win over the Redskins in their pre-season opener might be a good sign of things to come, especially if their Monsters of the Midway could humble the Packers in Milwaukee.

Coach Lombardi wanted a win over the Bears just as much as he would in a regular season game. He also knew that the Bruins were still sour about losing to the Packers not just once in 1964 but twice in the regular campaign; in Green Bay, 23-12, and in Chicago, 17-3. Vince wanted to keep the winning streak going, but Papa Bear Halas could care less about the outcome of a meaningless pre-season contest. Ol' George hoped more for finding a regular quarterback to lead his team back to glory.

Lombardi got his wish. His Packers and Halas's Bears played a scoreless first quarter. Neither team could mount any offense in the first quarter. Almost trapped after fielding a punt late in the first frame, Elijah Pitts wrestled free of two Chicago defenders, turned the corner and streaked 24 yards to the Bears' 43. A tough 10 plays later big Jim Taylor crashed the line for a one-yard TD behind the blocking of left tackle Bob Skoronski.

Just three minutes later the Bears were forced to punt again by a stalwart Green Bay defense. Willie Wood took this one with an assist from Pitts who threw the first block to spring Willie from a handful of Chicago assassins. Herb Adderley led Wood down the field for 37 yards to the Chicago 47. The Packer offense then went to work. Tom Moore capped an eight-play drive with a one-yard dash.

A puny punt by Chicago kicker Bobby Joe Green bounced out of bounds on the Green Bay 44. The Packers flexed their muscles one more time before the half ended. Pitts finished the 56-yard drive with a two-yard dash outside left guard for the final touchdown of the half. Don Chandler converted on all three Packer scores, giving Green Bay a 21-0 lead at the end of the second quarter.

Neither team could score in the third period. Then the Packers finally got a drive going late in the quarter, which culminated with a 41-yard field goal by Chandler 57 seconds into the fourth.

Trailing 24-0, the Bears finally mounted some offense behind second year QB Larry Rakestraw, who tossed a nine-yard scoring strike to rookie Dick Gordon.

Seconds later, Tom Moore fumbled the ensuing kickoff but downed the ball in the end zone. On the first play, backup QB Zeke Bratkowski sent a floater 50 yards downfield to Bob Long who caught it in full stride, raced by defender J.C. Caroline, and ended the play scoring the Packers' final touchdown of the evening.

The Bears managed another touchdown before the final gun, and the Packers walked away a 31-14 victory.

In a post-game interview, Lombardi stated unequivocally how unimpressed he was with his team's performance.

"We didn't sustain anything very well. Neither team did." He compared the Packers play against the Bears to the previous game against the Giants. I didn't see much improvement."

He said he thought the team had done a lot better on the kicking game. The most important aspect of the contest was the outcome: the Packers had soundly beaten the Bears.

Next up for Lombardi's boys was a trip to Texas and a ruckus with the Dallas Cowboys in the Cotton Bowl. Green Bay clawed to a 9-0 lead at the half on one field goal by Paul Hornung and two treys from the foot of Don Chandler. The Cowpokes offense, having gotten no closer to paydirt than the Packers 48 in the first two frames, came to life in the third quarter for a pair of TDs, while holding the Pack scoreless. Chandler added another three in the final stanza, but it wasn't enough for Green Bay as the Cowboys plowed their way to one more touchdown late in the game. The final score was Dallas 21, Green Bay 12. This was first time the Packers lost to the Cowboys in regular season and pre-season games.

Lombardi was so upset by the way his club played in Texas that he waited until Monday before speaking to the press. He began the conference by announcing the release of three rookies and the trade of another. Cut were halfback Bill Symons and defensive backs Donnie Davis and Wally Mahle. Defensive end John McDowell was sent to the New York Giants for an undisclosed draft choice in the next draft.

Finally, the coach commented on the game with Dallas.

"We actually played a little better than I thought. We made more mental errors than anything else. The Cowboys are a good football team, but we made a lot of mental errors, not a lot but enough to beat us."

He went on to promise his team wouldn't make those same mistakes once the regular season began.

Game #4 for the Packers pre-season schedule was set for a Saturday night in the home of the NFL champion Cleveland Browns. *Associated Press* writer Jack Hand predicted the Browns would not repeat as division champs. His pick to win the East was St. Louis with Cleveland second. For first in the West, he declared the Packers would once more find themselves on top ahead of Baltimore and the remainder of the Conference. Time would tell.

Before a packed house of 83,118 paid customers, the Packers took on the Cleveland Browns. Rebounding from the previous week's fiasco in Dallas, a bristling Green Bay squad humbled the reigning NFL champions, 30-14. Lombardi's crew flashed an explosive attack, hammering home two TDs in the first half and one more in the second. Don Chandler did his part as well, connecting on three field goal attempts in the second half, while the Green Bay defense shut down the vaunted Cleveland offense.

Paul Hornung slashed over left tackle for his five-yard TD to get the scoring going and capping an eight-play drive to paydirt. Elijah Pitts, filling in for injured Tom Moore, scored from one yard out just before the end of the half, sending the Packers ahead, 14-7. Then the Pack took total control of the contest. Starting with Chandler's first trey of the day to raise the score to 17-7, a Bart Starr nine-yard pass to Boyd Dowler in the end zone upped the ante to 24-7 Green Bay. The Browns closed the gap with their second and final touchdown, 24-14. Chandler booted two more field goals to finalize the score, 30-14.

As might be expected, Lombardi was pleased with the manner in which his Packers dispatched the NFL champion Cleveland Browns. He evinced even greater satisfaction over the substantial role his youth movement played in the victory. The future looked great for Lombardi and his Packers.

With only one more game in the pre-season, a Saturday night bout with the St. Louis Cardinals at Lambeau Field, Lombardi reduced his roster by placing three rookies on waivers. Tight end Jim Thibert, defensive back Jerry Roberts, and offensive tackle Rich Koeper were cut to lower the number of players to 43. Lombardi still had one more reduction to make to pare the squad to the league limit of 40. Going into the contest with St. Louis, the Packers still had 38 veterans and five rookies.

The game was highlighted by dedication ceremonies during which the stadium would be officially rechristened Lambeau Field in memory of the late Earl Louis Curly" Lambeau. Although he didn't found the city team that became the Packers and he didn't become the head coach of the team until the NFL granted him a franchise in the league in 1922, Curly was the driving force of professional football in Green Bay from 1918 thru 1949. If not for Curly and George Halas, who knows for certain that the National Football League would still be in existence. Their friendship and leadership kept the league alive through three decades that included the Great Depression of the 1930s, World War II, and competition from several leagues named the American Football League and the All-American Conference of the late 1940s. Lambeau and Halas came together to find an owner for an NFL team in New York City, the New York Giants who came into the league under the guidance of Tim Mara and his partner Will Gibson in 1925. Halas agreed to schedule two games against the Giants; one in each city. The game in New York drew an official 68,000 spectators, although estimates at the time for attendance was 73,000. The revenue from that one game saved the Giants from bankruptcy. That game not only saved the Giants, it also gave credence to the NFL over the AFL.

At the actual ceremony before the game against the St. Louis Cardinals, legendary end and defensive back Don Hutson climaxed the ceremony with an address to the sellout crowd of 50,858.

> ***"As you all know, Curly was always the eternal optimist. But even he could not predict a situation like this tonight." He briefly traced the history of the Packers since their beginning and said the team and the city have now reached the point where Green Bay is a very substantial part of the professional football world."***

Also speaking during the ceremony were Packer president Dominic Oleniczak and Clarence Nier, Green Bay city attorney and president of the city's stadium commission. Mayor Donald Tilleman officially dedicated the stadium to Lambeau's honor, presenting framed copies of City Council resolutions to Don Lambeau, Curly's only child. Don then made a brief address to the crowd.

> ***"I would be less than candid if I did not say that I am deeply moved by this occasion and that I shall be forever grateful for the opportunity to participate in it. It has often been said that my father was without sentiment, but those of you who knew him intimately, either as neighbor or friend or business associate, know that he, too, could not have stood here tonight without having been deeply touched. Speaking for all the Lambeaus, past, present, and those of the future, I want to thank all Packer fans, and the people of Green Bay in particular, for the generous recognition you, on this night, have accorded him for his fierce dedication to this team and to this town, his town and mine."***

A giant searchlight played across the eastern edge of the stadium, outlining the three-foot letters spelling out Lambeau Field, home of the Green Bay Packers."

As soon as the ceremony concluded, the Packers and Cardinals took the field to play the last pre-season game for both teams.

The Packers broke one of the strongest defenses in the NFL with four touchdown passes and a field goal, producing a hard-earned 31-13 victory over St. Louis. With the score tied at three points apiece, Paul Hornung threw 30 yards to Marv Fleming to up the score to 10-3. Then Bart Starr connected on a seven-yard TD to Boyd Dowler in the second quarter to make the score 17-6 at the half. Starr pitched his next touchdown pass five yards to Hornung in the third period to increase the lead to 24-6. Max McGee caught the final six-pointer from Starr, a 17-yarder to ice the game.

After the game, Lombardi was all smiles, saying,

"I would say we played about the same as we did against Cleveland, although I don't think we moved the ball as well."

♦♦♦

While NFL teams were still playing pre-season games, the AFL kicked off its 1965 season with a Saturday contest between the league champion Buffalo Bills and the Boston Patriots in Buffalo before a record crowd of 45,502 rabid fans. Buffalo came away with the victory, downing Boston, 24-7.

Also on Saturday night, Western Division champ San Diego Chargers nipped the Denver Broncos, 34-31.

On Sunday, the Houston Oilers opened their campaign at home against the New York Jets in front of a record crowd at Rice Stadium. A total of 52,680 spectators watched the home team slip by the Gotham City eleven, 30-21. Out West, Oakland smashed the Kansas City Chiefs, 37-10.

The total attendance for the four games was 143,863, another AFL record.

AMERICAN FOOTBALL LEAGUE STANDINGS FOR 1965									
EASTERN DIVISION					WESTERN DIVISION				
	W	L	T	PCT.		W	L	T	PCT.
Buffalo	1	0	0	1.000	**Oakland**	1	0	0	1.000
Houston	1	0	0	1.000	**San Diego**	1	0	0	1.000
Boston	0	1	0	.000	**Denver**	0	1	0	.000
New York	0	1	0	.000	**Kansas City**	0	1	0	.000

♦♦♦

Veteran defensive tackle Dave Hanner retired from the Packers before the last pre-season game, handing his position over to rookie Rick Marshall. This cut the roster down to 42 players. Hanner then became a defensive line coach for the Pack.

Lombardi traded two-year veteran linebacker Gene Breen to the Pittsburgh Steelers for a draft choice in the future. This move lowered the roster to 41.

To get down to the necessary number of active players on

the roster to start the season, Lombardi placed rookie offensive lineman Eli Strand on waivers.

Lombardi's 1965 team consisted of five 10-year players, two nine-years, seven eight-years, two seven-years, three six-years, three five-years, no four-years, six three-years, eight two-years, and four rookies, making the average age of the players 26.2 years old. More than half the team was below the average. Lombardi was building a roster for the future. That era would begin in Pittsburgh on the 19th of September.

§ § §

7

The Opening Charge

A veteran of nine years Bart Starr was more than ready to start the new campaign. He passed more in this year's pre-season games than he had in earlier exhibition contests. Was this a sign of things to come in 1965? Only time would tell.

Green Bay's first opponent of the new season was Pittsburgh. Coach Lombardi had been looking forward to matching wits with the Steelers head man Buddy Parker because the Pitt coach had won three Western Division titles and two NFL crowns when he was with the Detroit Lions in the early 1950s. Sadly, Parker tossed in the towel in Pittsburgh on Sunday September 5, handing over the coaching job to his top aide Mike Nixon who had been a star for the University of Pittsburgh in the 1930s and had played for the old Brooklyn Dodgers and the Chicago Cardinals. Nixon had served as head coach of the Washington Redskins in 1959 and 1960, but like so many previous head coaches before him, he ran afoul of owner George Marshall when his record in the Capitol was a sad 4-18-2. In Pitt's final pre-season game, Nixon's team fell to the Cleveland Browns, 28-16, in a contest played in Akron, Ohio.

Art Daley, Sports Editor for the Green Bay *Press-Gazette* had this to say about Pitt prior to the season opener. The Steelers have had umpteen coaches in their 33-year history … and hundreds of players have worn the Black and Gold. But one thing hasn't changed … the Steelers are hard-nosed, sticky, and always dangerous."

Pittsburgh sports writers used to call old Forbes Field the coal hole" because the Steelers loved to get contenders in there and smoke 'em up a bit. The smoke has been removed from Steeltown, and now the Steelers play high on a windy hill in the sanctity and purity of Pitt Stadium, which sits atop of what is known as Cardiac Hill.

Don Chandler, Green Bay's regular kicker, had this to say about playing in Pitt Stadium when he was with the New York Giants

> ***"We played them twice a year in the Eastern Division ... and they've always been a rock 'em sock 'em team. Pittsburgh always had good defensive teams, and that's what makes them hard-nosed."***

The last time the Packers played in Pittsburgh was 1960. Paul Hornung kicked four field goals in a tough 19-13 victory. The 1965 contest was almost as close—in the first half.

Just as Chandler had said, the Steelers' defense was tough as rusty nails in the first half, holding the Packers to a single touchdown, a 29-yard pass interception by Herb Adderley with a minute and 52 seconds left in the first half. The Packers did their share of defending their goal line in the first 30 minutes. Pitt kicker Mike Clark connected on three field goals, the last one just 12 seconds before the gun.

The second half was totally different. In the third period, Bart Starr connected with Marv Fleming for 32-yard TD pass to put the Pack ahead, 14-9. Chandler made good on two field goal tries to bump the third quarter score up to 20-9.

Starr threw another touchdown pass early in the final frame, this one a 10-yarder to Paul Hornung.

On Green Bay's next two possessions Elijah Pitts checked in with a pair of sixes; a two-yard run 5:53 into the quarter and a run of three yards two minutes later.

Starr was superb as usual, completing 17 of 23 passes for 226 yards. Jim Taylor gained 42 yards on 10 carries. Hornung had 11 carries for 50 yards to lead the ground attack. Tom Moore had 19 yards on four carries. Junior Coffey made 15 yards on a pair of runs.

Boyd Dowler led the pass receivers with six snares for 104

yards. Marv Fleming had 61 yards on four receptions. Carroll Dale pulled down four passes for 52 yards.

Adderley intercepted two Pitt passes. Ray Nitschke grabbed one from his linebacker position. Rick Marshall recovered one fumble.

The final score was 41-9 Packers.

In his after-game press conference, Lombardi confessed his team was:

> ***"sluggish out there in the first half, but we didn't decide on any changes at the halftime. The answer was getting to Pittsburgh QB Bill Nelsen in the second half, and we were able to do that." Ol' Vince added a laugh. I'm glad there are two halves to every football game." Then he considered the temperature for the game. It's hard to play in this kind of heat, but I think the weather bothered them more than us."***

How hot was it? 94 degrees and high humidity. Weather similar to training camp in Green Bay. The coach knew exactly how to get his boys prepared for the early season. Next on the schedule? Baltimore's Colts in Milwaukee.

♦♦♦

In the rest of the NFL, the San Francisco 49ers spanked the Chicago Bears, 52-24, in Frisco. The Dallas Cowboys stuck it to the New York Giants, 31-2, down in Big D. Cleveland humbled Washington, 17-7, in our nation's Capital. Detroit stuck it to Los Angeles, 20-0, in the Motor City. The Colts snuffed out the Vikings, 35-16, in Baltimore. In a real barn burner, Philadelphia slipped by St. Louis, 34-27, in Quaker Town.

NATIONAL FOOTBALL LEAGUE STANDINGS FOR 1965									
EASTERN CONFERENCE					WESTERN CONFERENCE				
	W	L	T	PCT.		W	L	T	PCT.
Cleveland	1	0	0	1.000	Baltimore	1	0	0	1.000
Dallas	1	0	0	1.000	Detroit	1	0	0	1.000
Philadelphia	1	0	0	1.000	Green Bay	1	0	0	1.000
New York	0	1	0	.000	San Francisco	1	0	0	1.000
Pittsburgh	0	1	0	.000	Chicago	0	1	0	.000
St. Louis	0	1	0	.000	Los Angeles	0	1	0	.000
Washington	0	1	0	.000	Minnesota	0	1	0	.000

♦♦♦

In the AFL, the Chiefs slipped by the Jets, 14-10, spoiling Joe Namath's debut as the Jets starting QB and disappointing the Shea Stadium standing room only crowd of 53,658 on Saturday night. In the Sunday games, the Houston Oilers defeated Boston Patriots, 31-10; the Buffalo Bills downed the Denver Broncos, 30-15; and the San Diego Chargers topped the Oakland Raiders, 17-6.

AMERICAN FOOTBALL LEAGUE STANDINGS FOR 1965									
EASTERN DIVISION					WESTERN DIVISION				
	W	L	T	PCT.		W	L	T	PCT.
Buffalo	2	0	0	1.000	San Diego	2	0	0	1.000
Houston	2	0	0	1.000	Kansas City	1	1	0	.500
Boston	0	2	0	.000	Oakland	1	1	0	.500
New York	0	2	0	.000	Denver	0	2	0	.000

♦♦♦

The Baltimore Colts were the reigning champions of the Western Conference. They had every intention of repeating, no matter what the Packers, Lions, Rams, Vikings, 49ers, and certainly not the rebuilding Chicago Bears thought they could do to stop them in the 1965 campaign. Already, the Colts had beaten the Vikings, something they failed to do the year before in the season opener. With the Packers next on their schedule just like they were the previous year, the Colts had plans to jump on Green Bay. Coach Lombardi and his staff had other ideas.

Art Daley wrote in his story about the game,

> ***"Judging by those two openers against the Vikings, the current Colts must be better."***

Baltimore director of publicity Harry Hulmes pointed out three differences on this year's team.

> ***(1) Buzz Nutter, the Colt center on the 1958-59 championship teams, had been obtained from the Steelers and was now the No. 1 center, with the departure of injured Dick Szymanski.***
>
> ***(2) Lou Michaels had replaced the retired great Gino Marchetti at defensive left tackle.***
>
> ***(3) Dennis Gaubatz had replaced the retired all-pro linebacker and captain Bill Pellington.***

Other than those three changes, the Colts were the same team that had defeated the Packers twice the year before. Maybe they were better than the year before. The only way to find out was for the two teams to square off in County Stadium.

Of course, the Packers had some new wrinkles in their team as well. Lombardi's realignment of the offensive line created several interesting situations for the big tangle between the Pack and Colts. Bob Skoronski would be lining up at left tackle, Forrest Gregg at left guard, Ken Bowman at center, Jerry Kramer at right guard, and first year man Steve Wright at right tackle. How the Baltimore front four would match up against the Green Bay blockers was anybody's guess, although Lombardi had a hunch Gregg's new position just might put a real wrinkle in the Colts' defense.

Just a little side note here. The Milwaukee Braves played their last game in County Stadium on the Wednesday night before the Green Bay-Baltimore tussle. The Braves lost to the Los Angeles Dodgers in extra innings, 7-6. Stalwart Braves' fans cried at the loss of their team. Already, they were making plans to get an expansion franchise in the Cream City. None would bear fruit for five years when the first Seattle team was purchased and moved to Milwaukee in 1970. The new team was appropriately named the Brewers.

The big game between the Colts and Packers was scheduled for kickoff at 1:05 p.m. Both teams were primed for a major battle.

And a battle it was. Baltimore did everything right to win the game, while the Packers made lots of mistakes. Green Bay registered a meager 184 yards, while the Colts piled up 309. Lombardi lost both Bart Starr and Paul Hornung in the third quarter. The Pack also lost a trio of fumbles and went into the final period trailing, 17-13. Backup QB Zeke Bratkowski and receiver Max McGee pulled a rabbit out of their helmets when McGee zigged one way then zagged another to catch a bullet from Bratkowski, then raced into the end zone with less than three minutes to go in the game. It was McGee's only reception in the game.

Then the Pack defense clamped down on the Baltimore offense at the perfect time. Herb Adderley recovered a Tom Matte fumble on the Pack's 23-yardline with just 56 seconds left.

Green Bay came away with an exciting victory, 20-17.

Tom Moore, filling in for the injured Jim Taylor, picked his way to 64 yards on 17 carries on the ground. Bratkowski completed just five passes in 19 tries. Adderley snared two of Johnny Unitas's throws. Ray Nitschke, Tom Brown, Willie Wood, and Adderley each recovered a Baltimore fumble.

Colts' coach Don Shula dourly declared at the post-game press conference,

> ***"I thought we gave them the ball game. They should be real appreciative."***

Lombardi was appreciative.

> ***"It was a great win for us, and we needed it. We lost a couple like this last year. It's about time something came our way."***

Off to an excellent start, the Packers went back to Green Bay on a Greyhound bus full of joy. Two down and 12 weeks to go. Good start, guys!

♦♦♦

Around the rest of the NFL that second Sunday of the season, the Bears blew a 28-9 lead in the 4th quarter, allowing the Rams 21 points and lost, 30-28, in Los Angeles. In Minneapolis, the Vikings also gave up the winning touchdown to the Lions in final seconds, and Detroit came away with a 31-29 victory. A crowd of 80,161 in Cleveland went home in tears because their Browns were snuffed by St. Louis, 49-13, as Cardinal QB Charley Johnson threw six touchdown passes. Out West, the 49ers took down the Steelers, 27-17. Down in Big D, those rising Cowboys ripped the Redskins, 27-7, on the shoulders of speedy wide receiver Bullet Bob Hayes who caught a TD pass and ran for another. In Philadelphia, the Giants slipped one over on the Eagles with a late field goal and came away with a 16-14 victory.

NATIONAL FOOTBALL LEAGUE STANDINGS FOR 1965									
EASTERN CONFERENCE					WESTERN CONFERENCE				
	W	L	T	PCT.		W	L	T	PCT.
Dallas	2	0	0	1.000	Detroit	2	0	0	1.000
Cleveland	1	1	0	.500	Green Bay	2	0	0	1.000
New York	1	1	0	.500	San Francisco	2	0	0	1.000
Philadelphia	1	1	0	.500	Baltimore	1	1	0	.500
St. Louis	1	1	0	.500	Los Angeles	1	1	0	.500
Pittsburgh	0	2	0	.000	Chicago	0	2	0	.000
Washington	0	2	0	.000	Minnesota	0	2	0	.000

♦♦♦

In the AFL, the Kansas City Chiefs and San Diego Chargers scrapped to a 10-all tie. The Houston Oilers lost their first game to Oakland in a close encounter, 21-17. Buffalo remained undefeated as the Bills handed the Jets their third loss of the season. Denver and Boston had the week off.

AMERICAN FOOTBALL LEAGUE STANDINGS FOR 1965									
EASTERN DIVISION					WESTERN DIVISION				
	W	L	T	PCT.		W	L	T	PCT.
Buffalo	3	0	0	1.000	San Diego	2	0	1	1.000
Houston	2	1	0	1.000	Oakland	2	1	0	.667
Boston	0	2	0	.000	Kansas City	1	1	1	.500
New York	0	3	0	.000	Denver	0	2	0	.000

♦♦♦

Now as one of three undefeated teams in the Western Conference, the Packers were more than excited to be hosting the always dangerous Chicago Bears in Lambeau Field in Week 3. In Lombardi terms, the battle with the Monsters of the Midway would happen in Bear Week 2 of 1965. He was already salivating over the chance to take Halas's boys to the woodshed. Now if he could only put that attitude into his more youthful players …

As for the red-faced Bears—red-faced because they had been creamed by the 49ers in their season opener and then blew a 19-point lead in the fourth quarter of their game against the Rams a week later in LA—Chicago's advance man Dan Desmond had all sorts of excuses for Papa Bear's cubbies. Cubbies? What better word to describe Ol' George's players so far that season?

Desmond ended his whine by saying, Halas feels that the current club is better than the 1964 team." Wow, Danny boy! Is that the best you can say about your Bruins? Apparently.

Another side note. Herb Adderley was chosen Defensive Player of the Week. The former Michigan State halfback raced 44 yards for a touchdown in the second period against the Colts by grabbing a Unitas pass intended for Jimmy Orr. Adderley also picked off a pass in the first quarter and ran it back 42 yards to the Baltimore 41. In the final frame, he recovered a fumble by Tom Matte. That's three turnovers in one game; something that doesn't happen all that often in pro football.

Good pregame news for the Packers. In the week's final full practice on Thursday, Jim Taylor, who had been held out of the game with Baltimore, Boyd Dowler, Paul Hornung, and Bart Starr were all declared fit for a fight with the Bears. Later, Lombardi confirmed that Starr and Hornung would play, but he declared that Taylor and

Dowler were still doubtful.

The coach also said he was a little eager to see Halas's pair of All-Americans in action. Dick Butkus and Gale Sayers had seen some action in their first two pro games, but neither man had made anything close to a dent in the outcome of Chicago's first two games. Halas promised that would change in due time. Maybe even in the first game against the Packers this season. Time would tell.

Lombardi knew an expression that sometimes fit professional football.

> ***"The most dangerous animal in the wild is a wounded bear."***

Or something like that. He hoped and prayed this would not be the case come Sunday in Lambeau Field.

If you looked at the game stats in the newspaper before finding the final score in the headline, then you just might think the Bears came away with a victory. Chicago had 23 first downs to Green Bay's 14. The Bears racked up 413 total yards to the Pack's 299. Chicago completed 17 of 29 passes, while the Packers only completed 11 of 20. You stare at those numbers, and you absolutely must believe the Bears got their first win of the season, and the Packers lost for the first time in 1965. Then you look up at the scoreboard. Green Bay 23, Chicago 14. The difference in the game? Lombardi's boys dominated the first half, 20-0, and the players from Halas Hall didn't get on the board until the Packers had a 23-0 lead on them early in the third quarter. The lesson here? Only points count in sports, not statistics.

The Pack did come out roaring like they usually did in most games since Lombardi took the team's reins in 1959. Being a genius at calling plays was only one aspect of his ability. More importantly, he knew how to fire up his boys in the locker room before they took the field. In this case, the Bears weren't just wounded in their first two games; they were shot dead by the 49ers and Rams. The Pack simply cut off their heads and mounted them on Lambeau Field's scoreboard.

With just 20 seconds left in the first quarter, the Packers got on the scoreboard, 7-0. Paul Hornung took the ball into the end zone on a one-yard dive. Junior Coffey upped the lead to 14-0 when he swiped a pass from Rudy Bukich and scampered 42 yards to paydirt as the period came to an end. Bobby Long hauled in a pass from Bart Starr for a 48-yard TD with 3:31 left on the clock before halftime, giving Green Bay a 20-0 lead. Don Chandler added a 16-yard FG early in the third frame to cap the scoring for the Packers.

Chicago finally managed to put some points on the board with a mere 38 seconds left on the third quarter clock. Gale Sayers found the end zone on a six-yard sprint. Sayers then capped the scoring with a mere 18 seconds left in the game when he hauled in a Bukich pass and raced 65 yards to make the final, 23-14.

After the game, Lombardi said sardonically,

> ***"I guess we felt we had a couple of touchdowns, and we could take a vacation. This is still a game of emotions, of hitting. You can't expect the other team to fall down. They're just not going to (do that). We did nothing in the second half. I can't be satisfied with that. I'm satisfied we won, but not with the way we played. The first half, I thought we played extremely well, but in the second ..."***

He could have said, The game was a tale of two halves. How else could you describe it?"`````````♦♦♦

Around the NFL that Sunday and Monday—yes, Monday; remember this time in Packer history happened in 1965, a most unusual time all over the world, starting with the Vietnam War—the Cleveland Browns crunched the Philadelphia Eagles, 35-17. Baltimore got back on the winning track by slipping by the 49ers, 27-24. Detroit stayed unbeaten by trimming Washington, 14-10. Minnesota slid into the win column with a 38-35 win over Los Angeles. The Giants downed the Steelers by a score of 23-13. And finally, on Monday night the Dallas Cowboys traveled to St. Louis and suffered their first loss of the year, 20-13, putting both teams in a four-way tie for first place in the Eastern Conference.

NATIONAL FOOTBALL LEAGUE STANDINGS FOR 1965									
EASTERN CONFERENCE					WESTERN CONFERENCE				
	W	L	T	PCT.		W	L	T	PCT.
Cleveland	2	1	0	.667	Detroit	3	0	0	1.000
Dallas	2	1	0	.667	Green Bay	3	0	0	1.000
New York	2	1	0	.667	Baltimore	2	1	0	.667
St. Louis	2	1	0	.333	San Francisco	2	1	0	.667
Philadelphia	1	2	0	.333	Los Angeles	1	2	0	.333
Pittsburgh	0	3	0	.000	Minnesota	1	2	0	.333
Washington	0	3	0	.000	Chicago	0	3	0	.000

♦♦♦

Week 4 in the AFL saw the Buffalo Bills remain undefeated as they downed Oakland, 17-12. Then San Diego stuck it to Houston, 31-14. Kansas City kept Boston in the loss column, 27-17. Denver did the same thing to the New York Jets, but barely, 16-13.

AMERICAN FOOTBALL LEAGUE STANDINGS FOR 1965									
EASTERN DIVISION					WESTERN DIVISION				
	W	L	T	PCT.		W	L	T	PCT.
Buffalo	4	0	0	1.000	San Diego	3	0	1	1.000
Houston	2	2	0	.500	Kansas City	2	1	1	.667
Boston	0	4	0	.000	Denver	2	2	0	.500
New York	0	4	0	.000	Oakland	2	2	0	.500

♦♦♦

Art Daley reported something very disturbing two days after the game with the Bears.

Although Lambeau Field was packed to capacity, he wrote,

> ***"... you could hear the proverbial pin drop, and like somebody asked in the press box, what's wrong with these people?"*** *(Author's italics.)*

Lombardi, while discussing the game with the media Monday afternoon, also brought up the quietness of the fans.

> ***"We received a perfunctory hand clap when we were introduced before the game. And the***

Bears got as much of a hand clap as we got. People are getting too satisfied. They are becoming blasé or maybe they think they are blasé."

Both sports editor and team coach implied the same thing. The fans in Green Bay had grown complacent about their team. Both men were more than worried that this complacency might rub off on the players and dampen their desire to win. Daley could do nothing about that, but Vince Lombardi sure as Hell could. He wasn't called the great motivator for nothing.

♦♦♦

Week #4 and the Packers were due to play hosts to the San Francisco 49ers in Lambeau Field.

The Packers came out of the Bear game with just one injury, Max McGee. Unfortunately, most of the receiving corps was already banged up. Boyd Dowler had an ankle injury. Carroll Dale had a pulled muscle that kept him out of the game. Dowler wasn't supposed to play either, but McGee's dislocated collar bone forced Lombardi to put Boyd in the game. This left one healthy flanker: sprightly sophomore Bob Long who made a decent showing against Chicago. Rumor had it that when he attended mass every morning that week, Lombardi asked the Lord for a miracle healing of his pass catchers.

San Francisco was known to have a solid offense, built around quarterback John Brodie, a passer supreme. The 49ers passing attack had already reached 811 yards in three games for an average of 270 per game. This was much better than all but one NFL quarterback: Charley Johnson of the Cardinals who had 849 yards for an average of 283 per game. Those were nice stats, but the one that counted the most was total points for the season. Frisco was the only team in the NFL to score more than 100 points so far with 103. The Packers were second with 84 points.

To go along with Brodie, the 49ers featured the rushing talent of rookie Ken Willard and veterans John Crow, Gary Lewis, and Dave Kopay. And there was the pass receiving of second year left end Dave Parks, veteran flanker Bernie Casey, and veteran tight end Monte Stickles, all three with sticky hands.

Frisco Coach Jack Christiansen, a future Hall of Famer, and like Lombardi, a real spitfire on the sidelines, inspired his players with a let-it-all-out attitude.

> ***"To hell with respect!" he told his players. We want to win."***

Come game day, the Packers were primed to play their best game yet this early in the season. They scored first, last, and three times in between. The 49ers scored twice. One touchdown and extra point in the second quarter, and one field goal in the third. Green Bay put all the pieces together for 60 minutes and came away with a 27-10 win to up their record to 4-0.

Jim Taylor led all rushers with 73 yards on 19 carries. His fellow back Paul Hornung gained 43 yards on nine carries. Elijah Pitts ran the ball three times for 29 yards. Don Chandler avoided getting a punt blocked by running with the ball for 27 yards and a first down. Chandler also set a record for punting, a 90-yarder. Bart Starr tucked the ball under his right arm and scooted 14 yards on his only carry.

Unfortunately, Starr's incredible record string of 294 passes without being intercepted came to a halt when Jim Johnson intercepted number 295 on the Frisco one-yard line in the second quarter. For the game, Starr completed 17 of 27 passes for 163 yards and a pair of TDs, one to Bob Long and the other to Hornung.

Boyd Dowler caught five passes for 46 yards. Long pulled down three for 48 yards. Marv Fleming snatched three for 23 yards. Hornung caught a pair for 25 yards. Carroll Dale two for 12 yards. And Taylor two for nine yards.

Coach Lombardi was more than happy with how his team played the entire game.

> ***"Don Chandler's run certainly was a big play, but those goal line stands were the keys—even the one on which the 49ers scored. They were tremendous. Our best overall effort of the season"—so far."***

The victory over San Francisco put the Packers in first place in the Western Conference all by themselves as well as making them the only undefeated team left in the entire league. Next up on the schedule a trip to the Motor City to face the now second place Lions.

♦♦♦

Around the NFL that Saturday night and Sunday afternoon—yes, Saturday night—the NFL was competing with the AFL for TV time— the Browns polished off the Pittsburgh Steelers, 24-19, on Saturday night in Cleveland. In the Midwest that same night, the Vikings were busy crushing the Giants in Minneapolis, 40-14. On Sunday, the Colts stomped the Lions in Baltimore, 31-7. In Chicago, the Bears finally get into the win column by spanking the Rams, 31-6, on the right arm and the speedy feet and legs of Gale Sayers. In Washington, D.C., the St. Louis Cardinals crushed the Redskins, 37-16. Finally, in Dallas, the Cowboys rode the legs of the fastest human in the world, Bob Hayes, to a 35-24 victory over the Philadelphia Eagles.

TIONAL FOOTBALL LEAGUE STANDINGS FOR 1965									
EASTERN CONFERENCE					WESTERN CONFERENCE				
	W	L	T	PCT.		W	L	T	PCT.
Cleveland	3	1	0	.750	Green Bay	4	0	0	1.000
St. Louis	3	1	0	.750	Baltimore	3	1	0	.750
Dallas	2	2	0	.667	Detroit	3	1	0	.750
New York	2	2	0	.500	Minnesota	2	2	0	.500
Philadelphia	2	2	0	.250	San Francisco	2	2	0	.500
Pittsburgh	0	4	0	.000	Chicago	1	3	0	.250
Washington	0	4	0	.000	Los Angeles	1	3	0	.250

♦♦♦

In the Friday AFL game between Oakland and Boston, the Raiders came away with a 34-10 win. In the Sunday games, San Diego knocked the Buffalo Bills from the unbeaten, 34-3, and the Kansas City Chiefs downed Denver, 31-23. The New York Jets and Houston Oilers had the week off.

AMERICAN FOOTBALL LEAGUE STANDINGS FOR 1965									
EASTERN DIVISION					WESTERN DIVISION				
	W	L	T	PCT.		W	L	T	PCT.
Buffalo	4	1	0	.800	San Diego	4	0	1	1.000
Houston	2	2	0	.500	Kansas City	3	1	1	.667
New York	0	4	0	.000	Oakland	3	2	0	.600
Boston	0	5	0	.000	Denver	2	3	0	.400

♦♦♦

The Lions took a beating from the Colts in Baltimore, putting both teams in a tie for second place in the Western Conference. Detroit's head man Harry Gilmer was determined not to let a loss like that happen again, especially to the Packers because that would drop the Lions another game deeper behind Green Bay.

For the first time this season, tight end Ron Kramer and wide receiver Gail Cogdill would be in the lineup together. Both men had great hands for catching a football. The pair posed a major problem for Green Bay's secondary.

On the other side of the ball, D-tackle Alex Karras presented a real problem for the Packers O-line. How to keep him away from Bart Starr like the Colts did for Johnny Unitas who said,

> ***"Please say they gave the (game) ball to Alex Sandusky. He's the one who earned it. He kept Alex Karras off me."***

Said Sandusky,

> ***"While I know that our offensive line had a good day, I don't feel like I dominated or even controlled Karras. When you play against a guy like Karras, you don't knock him down or drive him back. You just try to hold him off, keep him away from the passer. He's as quick as a cat and has a two-way move, meaning he can go to the inside or outside."***

This was the major issue for Green Bay. Detroit possessed one of the toughest defensive lines in the league. Karras, Darris

McCord, Sam Williams, and Roger Brown. Ringleader of this crew was Karras who was said to be having his best year. His teammates called him their 250-pound mosquito." Redskins coach Bill McPeak said,

> ***"He's the greatest (defensive) tackle in football. Most defense linemen have one or two moves. He has at least three. He's just a tremendous football player."***

Karras and Paul Hornung sat out the 1963 season due to their gambling mistakes. Both men suffered injuries in 1964 that limited their playing time. In the present campaign, both men were making big comebacks.

Jerry Kramer and Dan Grimm, who would be sharing the right guard position again in the coming game against Detroit, knew they would be facing Karras the whole afternoon. Neither man was looking forward to doing that.

All seemed good for the Packers going into the weekend. Then the bad news hit and hit hard. Forrest Gregg would be sitting out this game in the Motor City with a leg injury. Fuzzy Thurston would be taking his place, which was better than a rookie jumping in, but at this time in his career, Thurston was beginning to show signs of aging. The bossman on the sidelines could only hope and pray for the best.

To make matters worse, Lombardi revealed that Ray Nitschke and Boyd Dowler were in the doubtful" category for the game. Lee Roy Caffey would fill in for Nitschke at middle linebacker, and Tommy Crutcher would take Caffey's right linebacker spot. If Dowler couldn't go, Max McGee would fill in his spot.

The game turned out to be a tale of two halves. Detroit jumped ahead 21-3 in the first half, while the Packers came roaring back in the third quarter to take a 24-21 lead. Green Bay added seven more points in the final stanza and held the Lions scoreless to come away with a resounding 31-21 victory.

> ***"The Packers have pride," said a most jubilant Coach Vince Lombardi after the***

game. This was a great comeback. We stayed in there, and it paid off. This team has a great deal of pride, and the players knew they could come back."

And come back they did. The Packers scored 21 points in the third quarter behind a fabulous display of efficiency by Bart Starr. In the space of 13 plays, covering 13 minutes and 24 seconds, Green Bay's nerves of steel quarterback threw three touchdown passes, completed seven out of eight attempts for 249 yards, and called five rushing plays for 24 yards. To make matters worse for the Lions, Starr scored the final touchdown himself with a four-yard bootleg run.

Starr completed 15 of 23 passes for 301 yards and three TDs. The Lions did intercept him once. None of the Green Bay rushers had anything to brag about one the day. Pass receiving was good. Bob Long caught four for 106 yards. Carroll Dale hauled in three for 108 yards. Hornung snatched three for 27 yards. Taylor two for 18 yards. Moore, Fleming and Dowler caught one each for 31, eight, and three, respectively.

♦♦♦

The win over Detroit put the Packers in the NFL spotlight with a 5-0 record. All the rest of the Western Conference teams began rooting for Green Bay's next opponent, which happened to be the 2-3 Dallas Cowboys, losers to the Cleveland Browns, 23-17. In other games that week, Baltimore stayed close by whipping the Redskins, 38-7. The 49ers buried the Rams, 45-21. New York shot down the Eagles, 35-27. St. Louis handled the Steelers, 20-7. And the Bears outscored the Vikings, 45-37. Gale Sayers scored three touchdowns, one on a pass reception of 18 yards, another on a kickoff return of 96 yards, and the last one on a 10-yard sprint that finished off Minnesota. Sayers was named NFL Offensive Player of the Week for his performance. It wouldn't be his last. Right behind Sayers in the balloting was none other than Green Bay's Bart Starr.

NATIONAL FOOTBALL LEAGUE STANDINGS FOR 1965									
EASTERN CONFERENCE					WESTERN CONFERENCE				
	W	L	T	PCT.		W	L	T	PCT.
Cleveland	4	1	0	.800	Green Bay	5	0	0	1.000
St. Louis	4	1	0	.800	Baltimore	4	1	0	.800
New York	3	2	0	.600	Detroit	3	2	0	.600
Dallas	2	3	0	.400	San Francisco	3	2	0	.600
Philadelphia	2	3	0	.400	Chicago	2	3	0	.400
Pittsburgh	0	5	0	.000	Minnesota	2	3	0	.400
Washington	0	5	0	.000	Los Angeles	1	4	0	.200

♦♦♦

In the Saturday night AFL game between Oakland and New York, the Jets climbed out of the Eastern Division basement by tying the Raiders, 24-all. In the Sunday games, Denver spanked Houston, 28-17. The Buffalo Bills continued their winning ways by defeating Kansas City, 23-7. San Diego and Boston played kiss your sister" in a 13-13 tie.

AMERICAN FOOTBALL LEAGUE STANDINGS FOR 1965									
EASTERN DIVISION					WESTERN DIVISION				
	W	L	T	PCT.		W	L	T	PCT.
Buffalo	5	1	0	.833	San Diego	4	0	2	1.000
Houston	2	3	0	.400	Kansas City	3	2	1	.667
New York	0	4	1	.000	Oakland	3	2	1	.600
Washington	0	5	1	.000	Denver	3	3	0	.500

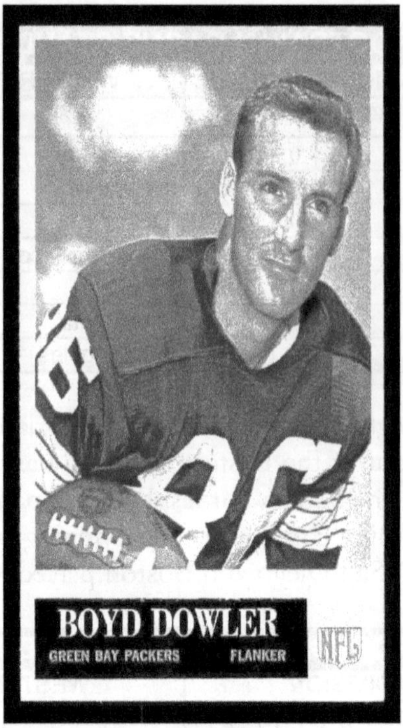

PHOTOS

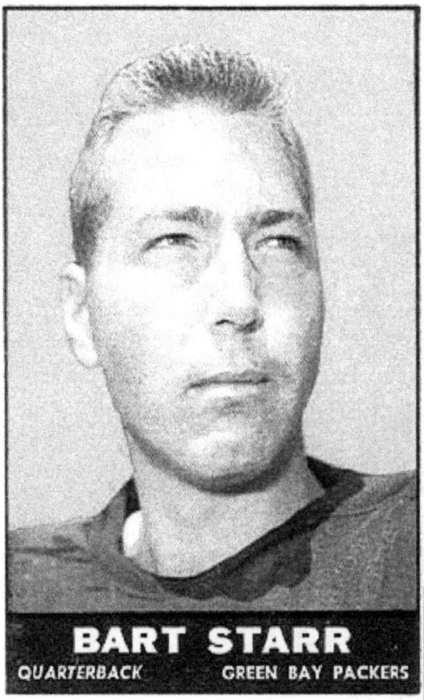

DON CHANDLER

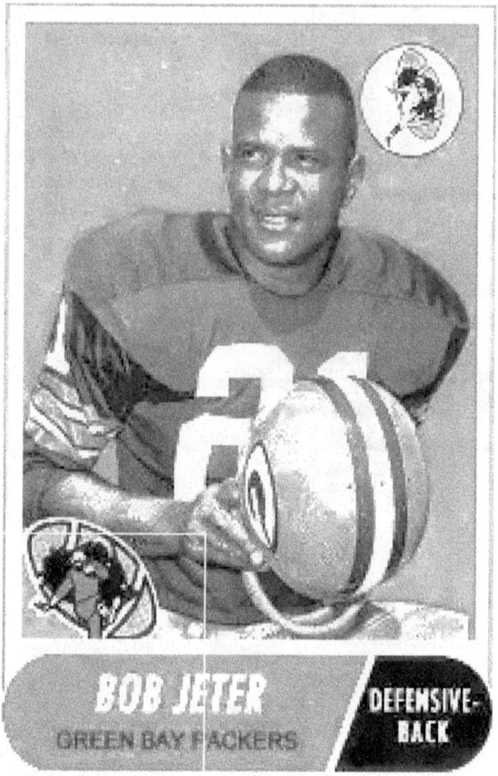
BOB JETER
GREEN BAY PACKERS
DEFENSIVE-
BACK

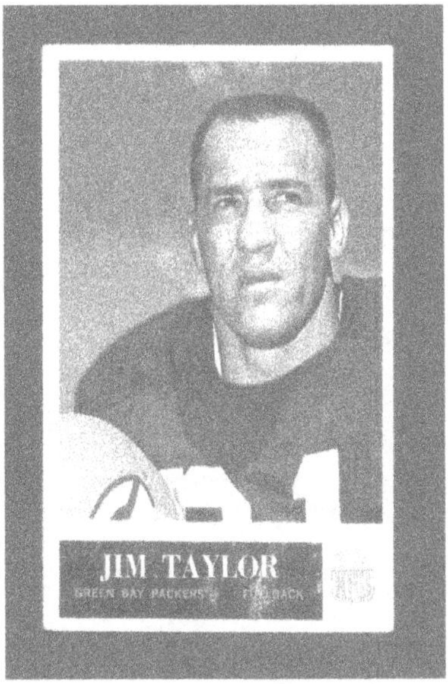
JIM TAYLOR

WILLIE DAVIS
GREEN BAY PACKERS
END
NFL

CARROLL DALE
PACKERS
WIDE RECEIVER

MAX
McGEE
GREEN BAY PACKERS
END

Triumphant Packers Return NFL Title to Green Bay

GREEN BAY PRESS-GAZETTE

Heavy Snow Hits State As Winter Lashes U.S.

Fans Fight Ice, Snow To Cheer Packer Win

Happy Fans Celebrate Long Into The Night

WILLIE WOOD

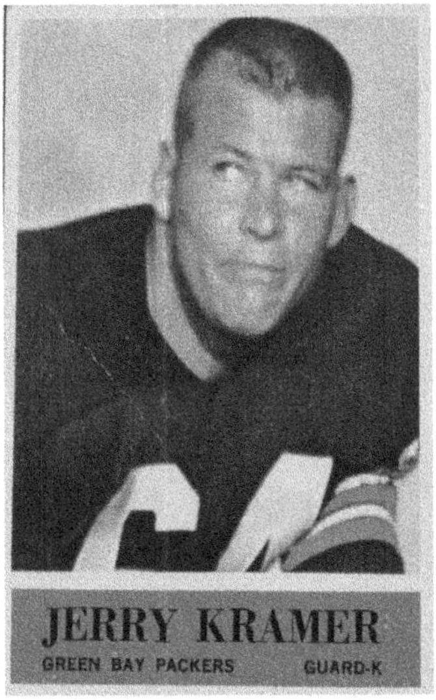
JERRY KRAMER
GREEN BAY PACKERS
GUARD-K

HERB ADDERLY
GREEN BAY PACKERS
HALFBACK

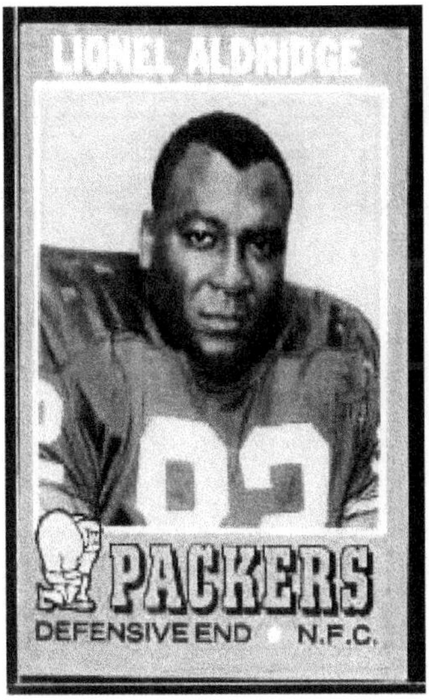
LIONEL ALDRIDGE
PACKERS
DEFENSIVE END
N.F.C.

Figure 1- Bart Starr with the football.

Figure 2- Jim Taylor carrying the football.

Figure 2 Ray Nitzke and Vince Lombardi.

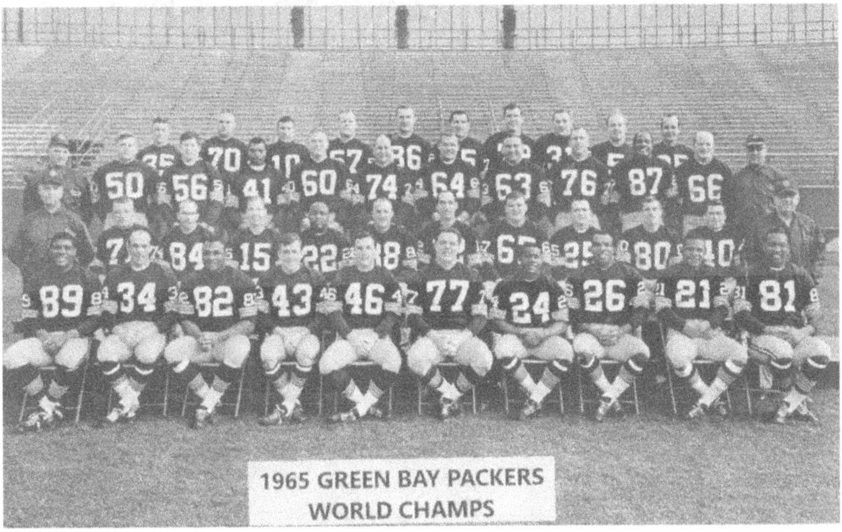

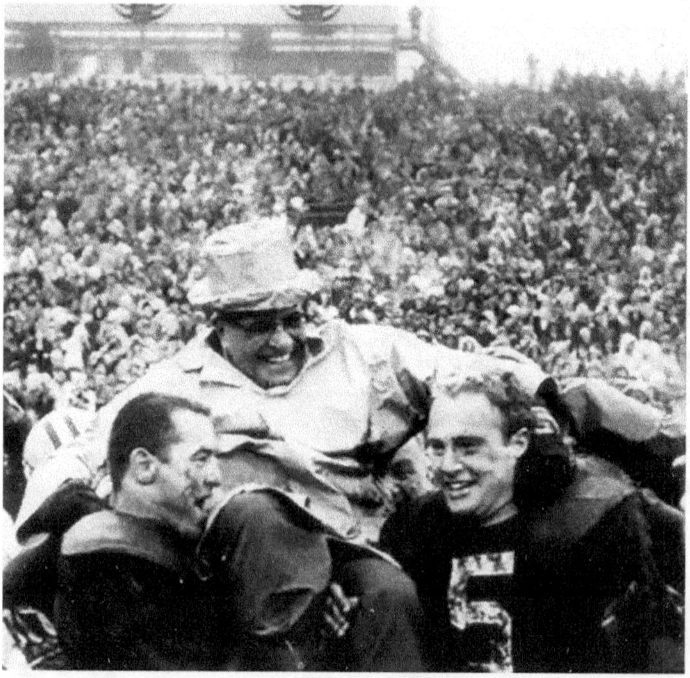

Figure 3- Vince Lombardi being carried from the field by Jim Taylor and Paul Hornung after the Packers win in the NFL Championship game against the Cleveland Browns on January 2, 1966.

§ § §

8

Five Down, Nine to Go

Most Packer fans thought their team had a firm grip on the Western Conference title with Green Bay's perfect record … thus far. That would have been totally acceptable if not for the fact that the Packers still had five road games remaining on their schedule. One each at Chicago, Minnesota, Baltimore, San Francisco, and Los Angeles.

However, their first game of the remaining nine was with the Dallas Cowboys at Milwaukee County Stadium. Remember how the boys from Big D handled the Packers in their pre-season encounter? Final score: Dallas 21, Green Bay 12.

That game still disturbed Coach Lombardi. He and his staff had to find a way to turn those four field goals they scored against the Cowboys into an equal number of touchdowns, if their Packers were to keep their undefeated season going strong.

The Dallas defense was led by the fantastic Bob Lilly at one tackle and captained by player-coach Jerry Tubbs at middle linebacker. An All-American from Alabama and a first-round draft pick in 1963, Lee Roy Jordan occasionally filled in for Tubbs.

To the Packers good luck, regular starting QB Don Meredith had been out of the lineup with a sore arm. Rookies Craig Morton and Jerry Rhome were trading off at quarterback, but for the game with Green Bay, Meredith was close to being healthy and was a possible starter. If Meredith couldn't go, then Dallas Coach Tom Landry would go with Morton as his starter in Milwaukee.

No matter who started under center, Landry's biggest weapon was the fastest human on Earth Bob Hayes. The Olympic dash man had accumulated 18 catches for 375 yards and four touchdowns. He was averaging 20.8 yards per reception. The question for the Packer secondary was, could they keep Hayes in their sights?

Well, Landry picked Morton to quarterback his team for the game against the Packers. Morton completed just 10 passes out of 20 for a minute total of 61 yards and none of his attempts were caught by Bob Hayes. Worse yet, two of those throws were intercepted, one by Tom Brown and a second by Willie Wood. Harder than that on Morton and his team, the Packer defense sacked him *nine* times. Even more devastating to the Cowboys were *three* lost fumbles, one each by Junior Coffey, Willie Davis, and Ron Kostelnik. The most important of those recoveries was that by Davis, who smothered his on the Dallas seven-yard line. On the next play, Starr handed the ball to Jim Taylor, and he busted his way into the end zone for the only touchdown in the game and giving Green Bay another win, 13-3.

As for the Packer offense, it practically failed to show itself that day. Paul Hornung gained 42 yards on eight carries. That was more than the combined yardage by Taylor (19 yards, 14 carries), Starr (nine yards, two carries), and Tom Moore (five yards, three carries).

And then there was Starr's passing. He threw 19 passes for 42 yards on a mere *four* completions.

Green Bay's coach had little to say about the win, but what he said was pure Lombardi..

> ***Our special teams were great—as was our defense. There are still two parts to this game, you know—offense and defense."***

Then a Milwaukee scribe imprudently suggested the offense hadn't been too impressive. Vince responded,

> ***"I don't give a damn about statistics as long as we win. I've told you many times statistics don't mean a thing. The important thing is whether you win."***

Another reporter asked, Would you say you were lucky?" To which he replied,

> ***"I don't think we were lucky. How can you say we were lucky? Our special teams caused them to fumble. ... Any time you hold anybody to three points, you've done a helluva job. ... It was a battle of defenses."***

And that was that. Vince. had spoken.

♦♦♦

Six weeks into the season now the standings were growing clearer and clearer as to which teams would still be in the hunt for the NFL title for 1965. Cleveland smothered New York, 38-14, to put a two-game lead over the Giants. St. Louis slipped a notch in the standings, losing to the Redskins, 24-20. Pittsburgh also pulled off an upset, slipping by Philadelphia, 20-14. In the Western Conference, the Bears won their third straight game, kicking the stuffing out of the Lions, 38-10, by riding on the passing arm of Rudy Bukich who completed 11 of 15 attempts for 120 yards and three touchdowns, one each to Johnny Morris, Gale Sayers, and Mike Ditka. Out West, Minnesota scrambled back three times on the legs of Fran Tarkenton to pull off a 42-41 win over the 49ers. The Baltimore Colts kept pace with the Packers at home against the hapless Los Angeles Rams. As usual, Johnny Unitas led a fourth quarter comeback by throwing two touchdown passes to Jimmy Orr. The first half put the Colts up 21-20, while the second finished off the Rams, 35-20. Unitas also ran for an 18-yard touchdown in the second period.

NATIONAL FOOTBALL LEAGUE STANDINGS FOR 1965									
EASTERN CONFERENCE					WESTERN CONFERENCE				
	W	L	T	PCT.		W	L	T	PCT.
Cleveland	5	1	0	.833	Green Bay	6	0	0	1.000
St. Louis	4	2	0	.667	Baltimore	5	1	0	.800
New York	3	3	0	.500	Chicago	3	3	0	.500
Dallas	2	4	0	.333	Detroit	3	3	0	.500
Philadelphia	2	4	0	.333	Minesota	3	3	0	.500
Pittsburgh	1	5	0	.167	San Francisco	3	3	0	.500
Washington	1	5	0	.167	Los Angeles	1	5	0	.167

♦♦♦

In the Saturday night AFL game, the Chargers pounded the Jets, 34-9. Between Oakland and New York, the Jets climbed out of the Eastern cellar. On Sunday, Oakland drubbed Boston, 30-21. Houston slipped by Kansas City, 38-36. And finally, Buffalo crunched Denver, 31-13.

AMERICAN FOOTBALL LEAGUE STANDINGS FOR 1965									
EASTERN DIVISION					WESTERN DIVISION				
	W	L	T	PCT.		W	L	T	PCT.
Buffalo	6	1	0	.833	San Diego	5	0	2	1.000
Houston	3	3	0	.500	Oakland	4	2	1	.667
New York	0	5	1	.000	Kansas City	3	3	1	.500
Boston	0	6	1	.000	Denver	3	4	0	.429

♦♦♦

Next on the menu for the Packers was a trip to Chicago to play the improved Bears in Wrigley Field. Lombardi had this to say about Bear Week #3.

> ***"They are a rejuvenated team. Their defense looks like the defense they had in 1963, and they'll be the most improved team we've faced thus far."***

Outright defensive battles were rare in pro football in the

mid-1960s because passing the pigskin was becoming more prevalent as each team's major weapon. The Bears and Packers fought one of those defensive battles back in Lombardi's historic debut as head coach of the Pack. Chicago came to town to open the 1959 season. The Bears managed a pair of field goals to take the lead, 6-0. Then Jim Taylor ripped around left end from five yards out to tie the game. Paul Hornung kicked the PAT to put the Packers ahead, 7-6. Then Dave Hanner and Henry Jordan nailed Chicago's QB Ed Brown in the end zone to seal the final score and Lombardi's first victory, 9-6.

In his weekly column on Wednesdays, the *Press-Gazette*'s Art Daley wrote a fascinating piece titled

RBs Pose Problems For Pack— Both Ways."

The RBs" were the initials for two Chicago players: Rudy Bukich and Richard Dick" Butkus.

The No. 1 QB in the NFL after Week 6 Bukich presented a problem for the Packer defense. Bukich had connected on a dozen TD passes and had completed 66 of 108 pass attempts for a glossy 61.1 completion percentage. In their previous meeting on October 3, Rudy entered the game in the second half and tossed a pair of touchdowns. The question facing the Packers was simple: What would Bukich do if he played all four quarters?

As for Chicago's rookie middle linebacker, Butkus received the game ball for his performance against the Lions in Week 6. A native of Chicago he was rewarded for his overall performance. He recovered two fumbles and intercepted a pair of passes.

"Butkus is a great player," said Chicago coach George Halas, and he gets better every week."

A third RB" on the Chicago roster was Ronnie Bull who just happened to have the best rushing average among Bears runners at 6.36 yards per carry.

Although his initials were totally different, Gale Sayers was leading the league in kickoff returns with an average of 36.7 yards per carry. The swift running back and pass catcher Sayers was also tied with Fred Cox, the placekicker for the Vikings, for the top spot in scoring with 54 points on nine touchdowns.

The top worry for the Packers was Chicago's winning streak of three straight games. Lombardi and company knew that a team on a hot streak was dangerous, especially on their home field, which was Wrigley Field on Chicago's North Side.

But how good did the Packers have to be to sweep the Bears a third time that year? Daley said it in a nutshell.

> ***"They'll have to be at their absolute best. They'll have to lift the defense they showed against the Cowboys and the offense they displayed against the 49ers—and apply both for four quarters. This is logical ... but there's something UN-logical about playing the Bears—especially in Chicago."***

Daley hit the proverbial nail on the head.

The Packers scored the first touchdown of the day in the first quarter. Green Bay took the opening kickoff 69 yards down the field that Jim Taylor finished off with a one-yard plunge into the end zone. The drive took six and a half minutes.

Then the Green-and-Gold defense held the Bears in check for the remainder of the period and led Chicago, 7-0.

The second stanza was a whole different game. Roger Leclerc, Chicago's placekicker, put a 24-yard chip shot through the uprights to get the Bears on the board just 50 seconds into quarter. The Pack still led, 7-3, at that point. A stalemate followed for several minutes. Then what could go wrong went wrong—terribly wrong—for the visiting team.

A Bart Starr pass deflected off someone's helmet and into the huge hands of Doug Atkins, Chicago's vicious D-end. The turnover put a real damper on the Pack, but worse, it lit a fire under the Bears offense. In four plays, Chicago moved the ball 43 yards to paydirt, the final nail in that coffin being a 13-yard pass from Rudy Bukich to wide receiver Jimmy Jones, a graduate of the University of Wisconsin. This score put the Bears ahead, 10-7, with three minutes and nine seconds to go in the half. Starr then overshot Boyd Dowler, and Chicago DB Bennie McRae pulled in the errant pass. Three plays later from the Bears' 31 Sayers scored from the Green Bay 10 to raise Chicago's lead to 17-7. Finally, the Packers managed to get into field goal range for Don Chandler to boot a 43-yarder to make the halftime score 17-10 in favor of Chicago.

In the second half, the Packers could do little to nothing. The offense put up a goose egg, and the defense gave up two more Bear touchdowns, one in each quarter, to seal the game for the Monsters of the Midway, 31-10.

Stat wise, Starr had a better game this week than he had the previous Sunday against Dallas. He completed 10 of 20 attempts, 13 of 20 if you count the three Chicago interceptions. Taylor had a so-so game with 50 yards on 16 runs. Starr was the best rusher for the Pack with 46 yards on just three carries. The rest of the ground attempts netted a total of 23 yards on 16 rushes.

Lombardi summed up the game succinctly at the end of his post-game press conference.

> ***"The Bears blocked better, ran better, and they passed better—and they defensed us better. That's all there was to it." In conclusion, he barked, What the hell do you want me to say? You're trying to make a mountain out of a molehill."***

Around the NFL, the Lions traveled to Los Angeles where the Rams gifted them with five fumbles for Detroit to recover as they blew out the LA entry, 31-7. Back in New York, the Giants came back from a first half deficit of 10-0 to beat the Cardinals, 14-10. Out on the West Coast again, the 49ers came up short against Baltimore, 34-28, and the Colts moved into a first-place tie in the conference with Green Bay. Jumping to the East Coast again, Sonny Jurgensen led the Redskins to another upset, this one over the Eagles, 23-21. Not to be embarrassed with last place by themselves, the Steelers pulled off another upset of their own by downing Dallas, 22-13. The final game of Week 6 had the Vikings showing some real defense by holding Cleveland to only 34 yards rushing the ball and outscoring the Browns, 27-17.

NATIONAL FOOTBALL LEAGUE STANDINGS FOR 1965									
EASTERN CONFERENCE					WESTERN CONFERENCE				
	W	L	T	PCT.		W	L	T	PCT.
Cleveland	5	2	0	.714	Baltimore	6	1	0	.857
New York	4	3	0	.571	Green Bay	6	1	0	.857
St. Louis	4	3	0	.571	Chicago	4	3	0	.571
Dallas	2	5	0	.286	Detroit	4	3	0	.571
Philadelphia	2	5	0	.286	Minesota	4	3	0	.571
Pittsburgh	2	5	0	.286	San Francisco	3	4	0	.429
Washington	2	5	0	.286	Los Angeles	1	6	0	.143

♦♦♦

The AFL games were all played on Sunday. Playing in front of a home field crowd of 53,717, the Jets wrangled the Broncos, 45-10, for their first win of the season. Houston upset the Bills in Buffalo behind the toe and arm of George Blanda who kicked four field goals and passed for one touchdown to lead the Oilers to victory, 19-17. Another big upset happened on the West Coast where Boston pulled off its first win of the year by downing the Chargers, 22-6. Kansas City pulled into a tie for second place in the West by defeating Oakland, 14-7.

AMERICAN FOOTBALL LEAGUE STANDINGS FOR 1965									
EASTERN DIVISION					WESTERN DIVISION				
	W	L	T	PCT.		W	L	T	PCT.
Buffalo	6	2	0	.750	San Diego	5	1	2	.833
Houston	4	3	0	.571	Kansas City	4	3	1	.571
New York	1	5	1	.167	Oakland	4	3	1	.571
Boston	1	6	1	.143	Denver	3	5	0	.375

♦♦♦

With their last Bear Week of the season behind them—behind them as long as the Windy City boys didn't tie them for first place in the conference and force a playoff game for the Western title—the Packers had their fate in their own hands. All they needed to do was win all seven of their games in the second half, one of which would be with the Colts on the road in Baltimore.

In the meantime, Lombardi and company had to contend with the Lions in Lambeau Field in Week 8 of the season.

The coach said firmly to Art Daley and the rest of the press covering the game in Chicago,

> ***"We're not pushing the panic button. One win doesn't make a season, and one loss doesn't lose it."***

Later, he admitted that the Bears were now in the race with Baltimore and Green Bay for the conference title.

That was Art Daley's theme when his Wednesday story about the Packers hit the newsstands.

"Champion in West? Could Be Pack, 4 Others."

Baltimore was now tied with the Packers for first place. Right behind them were Chicago, Detroit, and Minnesota, the last very quietly coming alive in the standings at the halfway point in the season. Anything could happen in the competitive Western Conference.

All seven teams in the West were still mathematically in the race, even the Rams who were 1-6. LA was not likely to win all seven of their remaining games, but miracles do happen in the sports world. One loss by the Rams would put them in the wait 'til next year" row or the next decade column. So, scratch the Rams from the race.

The 49ers were 3-4 in the first half standings. Five teams were ahead of them. Could they win all seven games? Possible but not very likely. Three losses would definitely put them out of the race.

That leaves the Bears, Lions, and Vikings, all three of them with 4-3 records. Chicago was on a four-game winning streak, with the fourth victory coming against the Packers. Lombardi said publicly that he hoped the Bears would do the same thing in their next game that they had done to his team. Chicago's next opponent?

The Colts in Wrigley Field.

The Lions planned to upset the Packers in Lambeau Field in the same manner in which Green Bay had handled them in Detroit. A win in Wisconsin would get the Kings of the Jungle back into the race for the conference crown.

Minnesota had been down and up so far in 1965. Losses to Baltimore and Detroit to start the season really rankled their leader Coach Norm Van Brocklin. His Vikings sheared the Rams in LA in the third week, then they clobbered the Giants in Minneapolis in game four before being upset by the Bears in week five on their own turf. Van Brocklin knew his team were masters of their own destiny as they headed into a four-game homestand. Win all four of those against the hapless Rams, the tough-as-bent-nails Colts, the also powerful Packers, and the up-and-down 49ers, and Minnesota would be 8-3 and quite possibly in the middle of the race for the Western Conference title with Baltimore and Green Bay.

Speaking of Baltimore, the Colts were on a five-game winning streak with four games on the road left on their schedule, starting with the Bears and then the Vikings, both of which were red hot. Those encounters were followed by a home game against Philadelphia, then Thanksgiving in Detroit, a date every visiting team hated to keep. Keeping their winning streak alive seemed quite possible to their boss man Head Coach Don Shula.

As for the Packers, Lombardi was already steaming over the loss to the Bears. No way did he want another thrashing like that one. Beat Detroit again. Hammer LA twice. Do the same to the Vikings. Take down Unitas and Company again. And finally, bury the 49ers in their own hole. After that, defeat the Eastern Conference champ and win the NFL title again. Simple, right? It would be, if the Packers could play nothing but losers the rest of the way.

♦♦♦

In a full-page ad in the *Press-Gazette*, the owner and his two managers of his liquor stores predicted the Packers would wipe the Lions' hind ends come Sunday. One predicted Packers 57, Lions 17. The second's prognostication was 45-10 in favor of the Packers. And the final swami predicted the final score would be Packers 38, Lions 14.

Maybe these gentlemen had been sampling their own merchandise when they put forth their prophecies. The final score was nothing near their guesses.

The real Packer news of that same day was written by Sports Editor Art Daley. He took great pleasure in reporting that Vince Lombardi's contract as head coach and general manager of the Green Bay Packers had been renewed and extended to January 31, 1974. This announcement was made early that day by Dominic Olejniczak", the president of the Green Bay Packers, Inc. This quashed all the rumors and reports that Lombardi would be taking over both positions with the new Atlanta franchise. The new deal was the third time Lombardi's contract was extended.

Lombardi could not be reached for comment when the news broke that morning. He was a little busy with preparations for the very important game with the Lions in Lambeau Field that Sunday.

Speaking of the Motor City team, Notre Dame Fighting Irish graduate George Izo started the previous week for the Lions against the Los Angeles Rams and led them to an impressive 30-7 victory. Izo had been in the NFL for six seasons, but he had only started in two games prior to the one against LA. The question before Sunday's game was simple. Would he start against the Packers?

Well, Izo started for the Lions, and he completed six out of 14 passes for 67 yards. Not exactly bad considering he was going up against one of the best defenses in the league. Trouble was he threw three interceptions. One each to Willie Davis, Willie Wood, and Tommy Crutcher. Izo did gain more net yards passing than Bart Starr, 52 to -2. Yes, minus two. Starr completed nine of 12 passes for 107. Paul Hornung and Elijah Pitts also threw the ball once each. Neither back completed his pass, and worse yet, Hornung's was intercepted.

Detroit's defense proved the better one for the day. The Lions sacked Starr 11 times for a total of 109 negative yards; thus, the minus two yards. The Packers did gain 70 yards on the ground, 50 of them by Jim Taylor on 14 carries. Pitts gained 15 on five carries. Hornung made a meager four yards on seven attempts.

Green Bay scored first on a one-yard plunge by Tayor with two minutes and 42 seconds left in the half. Detroit marched down the field to score their only touchdown of the game with just 15 seconds left in the period. Neither team could score a six-pointer in the game. In fact, the Packers were held scoreless for the remainder of the game, while the Lions booted a field goal in the fourth quarter with three minutes and 51 seconds left in the game. Two plays later Starr was tackled in the end zone by Detroit defensive tackle Roger Brown. That sealed the final score at 12-7.

Lee Remmel, sportswriter for the *Press-Gazette*, summed up the game in the words of Coach Lombardi.

> ***"Managing a wisecrack despite the pain, Vince Lombardi bravely quipped, 'It looks like a funeral procession,' as the press corps slowly filed into his Lambeau Field office Sunday afternoon."***

A downhearted Lombardi summed up the game succinctly.

> ***"They overpowered us all the way. That's the story of the game. That's the story of the game. Defensively, we played well enough—better than well enough—to win any ordinary game. He added, They overpowered our line all the way."***

♦♦♦

The Lions' victory kept them in pace with the Vikings, winners over Los Angeles, 24-13, the Packers' next opponent at County Stadium in Milwaukee. Unfortunately, the Bears could not do to Baltimore what they had done to the Packers in Week 7. The Colts came away with a win in Chicago, 26-21. In the Eastern Conference, Cleveland won again, 38-24, over Philadelphia. The Cardinals narrowly downed the Steelers in St. Louis, 21-17, staying in the race for the conference crown. Washington won again, taking down the Giants, 23-7. And the interconference game went to Dallas when the Cowboys scored first and last to defeat San Francisco, 39-31. Statistically, the 49ers pounded the Cowpokes, registering 26 first downs to Dallas's nine and 401 yards of total offense to Dallas's 243.

NATIONAL FOOTBALL LEAGUE STANDINGS FOR 1965									
EASTERN CONFERENCE					WESTERN CONFERENCE				
	W	L	T	PCT.		W	L	T	PCT.
Cleveland	6	2	0	.750	**Baltimore**	7	1	0	.875
St. Louis	5	3	0	.625	**Green Bay**	6	2	0	.750
New York	4	4	0	.500	**Detroit**	5	3	0	.625
Dallas	3	5	0	.375	**Minnesota**	5	3	0	.625
Washington	3	5	0	.375	**Chicago**	4	4	0	.500
Philadelphia	2	6	0	.250	**San Francisco**	3	5	0	.375
Pittsburgh	2	6	0	.250	**Los Angeles**	1	7	0	.143

♦♦♦

Nine weeks into their season the AFL races were narrowing down to Buffalo in the East and San Diego in the West. The Bills traveled to Boston and came away with a 23-7 win. Oakland took down Houston, 33-21, leaving the Oilers a game and a half behind Buffalo. San Diego stayed a game and a half ahead of the Raiders by dumping Denver's Broncos, 35-21. The Jets won for the second time, slipping by Kansas City, 13-10.

AMERICAN FOOTBALL LEAGUE STANDINGS FOR 1965									
EASTERN DIVISION					WESTERN DIVISION				
	W	L	T	PCT.		W	L	T	PCT.
Buffalo	7	2	0	.778	**San Diego**	6	1	2	.857
Houston	4	4	0	.500	**Oakland**	5	3	1	.625
New York	2	5	1	.286	**Kansas City**	4	4	1	.500
Boston	1	7	1	.125	**Denver**	3	6	0	.333

♦♦♦

Having lost two games in a row, the Packers felt totally glum to a man as they prepared to play the Los Angeles Rams, a team that beat them in Green Bay and tied them in LA the previous season. The Rams were no more than a mediocre team, but their coaching staff, led by Harlan Svare and known as The Swede around the NFL, they seemed to be working on creating a curse on Lombardi's boys.

Rams' publicity director Jack Teele indicated such when he addressed the *Mike and Pen Club* in Milwaukee. After the local audience settled down, he quickly changed course.

"We've been losing, too—six in a row, so what are you guys hollering about ... with only two in a row. We've had straight losing years of below .500, and we stand a good chance of making it seven. The defense got the Rams into trouble due to injuries, and right away we lost three linebackers for unusual reasons. Mike Henry retired to play Tarzan in the movies. Jack Pardee retired to coach, and the other starter from last year got cut.

We're going with three rookies at linebacker. Doug Woodlief in the middle and Fred Brown and Tony Guillory on the outside. They've been good. Enough to keep veterans Cliff Livingston, who has been hurt, and Dan Currie on the bench.

We have two rookies in the defensive backfield—Clancy Williams. and Dan McIlhany, and our only Ram veteran behind the line is Eddie Meador. The other back is Chuck Lamson, who was with the Vikings. Our best defensive back, Aaron Martin, broke his arm in Chicago.

Our front four (Lamar Lundy, Rosey Grier, Merlin Olsen, and David Deacon" Jones) was broken up most of the early part of the season. Lundy had surgery and missed the first three games, and Grier had a bad ankle. This unit is just now playing its best ball."

That last statement by Teele was the first one Lombardi took totally seriously. LA's defensive line was known as the Fearsome Foursome" in the NFL. Learning that they were all healthy, the Packer coach realized they could be as deadly as the Lions were in Week 8. His offense really had to prepare for those four demons come Sunday in Milwaukee.

The Packers had scored a grand total of 30 points and given up only 46 in their last three games against the Cowboys, Bears, and Lions. Lombardi hoped his offense would do much better against the Rams in Milwaukee.

Art Daley wrote humorously,

> ***"The Packer offense may be out in left field—at the moment, that is—but the Packer defense sure knows what to do in County Stadium's short left field."***

Offense out in in left field? Really, Art? The Green Bay offense was out in the left field bleachers for the last four games.

Lombardi's defense held the Rams to a single field goal, while the Packer offense managed two field goals and no touchdowns. The final score was set up by LA quarterback Bill Munson fumbling the ball and Lionel Aldridge recovering it. After six plays and the ball on the one-inch line, Don Chandler kicked his second field goal to win the game.

Stat wise, neither team did much of anything. The Packers had a net gain of 177 yards, 102 on the ground and 75 through the air. LA was worse with 142 net total yards, 116 on the ground and 26 passing.

Only Jim Taylor had a reasonable day bulldozing his way to 68 yards on 19 carries. He also caught two passes for 49 yards.

The Green Bay defense sacked Munson five times for 43 yards lost. Doug Hart intercepted one pass, while Dave Robinson, Willie Davis, and Aldridge each recovered a fumble.

Lombardi was very succinct when addressing the reporters after the game.

"Certainly, I'm happy with the victory. For the first time in three or four weeks our running game looked like it was coming, and Taylor was better than he has been all season."

♦♦♦

Baltimore continued its victorious ways by crushing the Vikings, 41-21. Minnesota coach Norm Van Brocklin, upset by the loss, turned in his resignation the next day. After cooling off, Stormin' Norman" came to his senses and returned to finish the season and coached the next year in Minnesota as well.

The Bears returned to the win column with a 34-13 romp over the Cardinals. San Francisco tamed the Lions, 27-21. Cleveland shrank the Giants, 34-21. The Cowboys wrangled the Steelers, 24-17, to pen them in the Eastern Conference cellar. Philadelphia shook up Washington, 21-14.

NATIONAL FOOTBALL LEAGUE STANDINGS FOR 1965									
EASTERN CONFERENCE					WESTERN CONFERENCE				
	W	L	T	PCT.		W	L	T	PCT.
Cleveland	7	2	0	.778	Baltimore	8	1	0	.889
St. Louis	5	4	0	.556	Green Bay	7	2	0	.857
Dallas	4	5	0	.444	Chicago	5	4	0	.556
New York	4	5	0	.444	Detroit	5	4	0	.556
Philadelphia	3	6	0	.333	Minesota	5	4	0	.556
Washington	3	6	0	.333	San Francisco	4	5	0	.444
Pittsburgh	2	7	0	.222	Los Angeles	1	8	0	.111

♦♦♦

In the junior league, Buffalo became a half game away from winning the Eastern Division crown when the Bills edged Oakland, 17-14. San Diego lost ground to Kansas City when the Chiefs beat the Chargers, 31-7. Denver put the kibosh on Houston, 31-21, to sink the Oilers another game behind the Bills. New York buried Boston deeper in the Eastern basement, 30-20.

AMERICAN FOOTBALL LEAGUE STANDINGS FOR 1965									
EASTERN DIVISION					WESTERN DIVISION				
	W	L	T	PCT.		W	L	T	PCT.
Buffalo	8	2	0	.800	San Diego	6	2	2	.750
Houston	4	5	0	.444	Kansas City	5	4	1	.556
New York	3	5	1	.375	Oakland	5	4	1	.556
Boston	1	8	1	.111	Denver	4	6	0	.400

♦♦♦

With the short losing streak over now, Lombardi heaved a sigh of relief because he knew his defense could be counted on to play well. Now, to get the offense back on track. A conference title could still be had. But, as the old saying goes, one game at a time, and next up for the Packers? The Minnesota Vikings and their questionable head coach Norm Van Brocklin.

Word had it that emotions seem to be mixed." Those feelings were based on what Tom Miller, Packers' publicist, who was advance man for Green Bay said. Fans in the Twin Cities were fairly divided about Van Brocklin resigning one day and taking back his resignation the next.

The bigger question concerned the attitudes of the Minnesota players. No one could know how those men felt about their coach's rather odd behavior.

Back in Green Bay, Lombardi was driving his offense harder than usual in preparation for the Vikings in Metropolitan Stadium in Minneapolis. Art Daley wrote that the coach was putting emphasis on the offense, particularly the offensive line protecting their quarterback as he set up to pass. After four weeks of a lousy performance by his line, who could blame Lombardi for driving his guys so hard?

For the first time since their inception in the NFL, the Vikings were favored by two points. This certainly lit a fire under the offense as well as the defense.

With the temperature hovering around freezing all afternoon, the Packers played like they were on fire. Minnesota put a three on the scoreboard first, then the Pack fired back with a touchdown toss from Bart Starr to Carroll Dale with 53 seconds left in the first quarter. Then Don Chandler connected on a 36-yard field goal midway through the second period. Minnesota added another three late in the half to make the score, 10-6, in favor of Green Bay.

Fran Tarkenton connected with Paul Flatley halfway through the third stanza to take the lead, 13-10. Then all Hell broke loose. For the visiting team.

Starr found Boyd Dowler for a 47-yard TD just 14 seconds into the final period. Chandler converted to give Green Bay the lead, 17-13. On their next possession, Elijah Pitts slipped through the line for three yards and another touchdown. Only 73 seconds later, Doug Hart picked up a Viking fumble and raced 20 yards into the end zone. Chandler converted again. Packers 31, Vikings still 13. Starr got his third TD pass into the hands of Bob Long from 11 yards out with 2:54 left on the clock. Neither team scored after that, and the Packers found themselves celebrating a 38-13 victory on the road.

Starr also threw two interceptions, but his completions were nine in number and 18 in points on the board, unless you count the extra points on his TDs, then it was for 21 points. Bart also ran for 44 yards on just a pair of carries. Jim Taylor led all rushers with 111 yards on 25 attempts. Boyd Dowler caught three passes for 78 yards. Tom Moore snared three as well for 50 yards. Dave Robinson and Herb Adderley each picked off an interception.

Lombardi credited Starr and Taylor for leading the way to a much-needed win. Of course, the coach cited the defense for holding back Fran Tarkenton from taking control of the game.

He's an amazing boy."

Baltimore continued its winning ways by downing Philadelphia, 34-24. The Bears stayed in the race with a 17-10 victory over Detroit. San Francisco slipped by Los Angeles, 30-27, creating a three-way tie for fourth place with Detroit and Minnesota. One more loss by any one of them would eliminate that team for the conference title. Cleveland's 24-17 win over Dallas moved the Browns within a single victory of clinching a tie for the Eastern crown. Washington crushed Pitt, 31-3. New York stayed alive in the chase by beating St. Louis, 28-15.

NATIONAL FOOTBALL LEAGUE STANDINGS FOR 1965									
EASTERN CONFERENCE					WESTERN CONFERENCE				
	W	L	T	PCT.		W	L	T	PCT.
Cleveland	8	2	0	.800	Baltimore	9	1	0	.900
New York	5	5	0	.500	Green Bay	8	2	0	.800
St. Louis	5	5	0	.500	Chicago	6	4	0	.600
Dallas	4	6	0	.400	Detroit	5	5	0	.500
Washington	4	6	0	.400	Min nesota	5	5	0	.500
Philadelphia	3	7	0	.300	San Francisco	5	5	0	.500
Pittsburgh	2	8	0	.200	Los Angeles	1	9	0	.100

♦♦♦

In the AFL, the two division leaders, Buffalo and San Diego, had the week off. Oakland held on to their hopes of winning their division by beating the hapless Broncos, 28-20. The Jets were getting better as they crushed Houston, 41-14. Kansas City and Boston played to a 10-10 tie.

AMERICAN FOOTBALL LEAGUE STANDINGS FOR 1965									
EASTERN DIVISION					WESTERN DIVISION				
	W	L	T	PCT.		W	L	T	PCT.
Buffalo	8	2	0	.800	San Diego	6	2	2	.750
New York	4	5	1	.444	Oakland	6	4	2	.600
Houston	4	6	0	.400	Kansas City	5	4	1	.556
Boston	1	8	2	.111	Denver	4	7	0	.364

♦♦♦

Vince Lombardi knew his team had a narrow chance of winning the Western Conference. Four weeks were left in the regular season. One more loss or a tie could mean disaster for the Packers. They could not play like they had been playing in the last four weeks. Dominate was the key word for them. Dominate! Or spend the winter, spring, and summer trying to figure out how to get better.

§ § §

9

Time for a Miracle

Baltimore continued to hold onto first place in the West. The Packers remained in second. Chicago still had a wing and prayer of catching both leaders. Every other team in the conference knew the season was basically over for them.

Vince Lombardi was a realist. He knew the most important game left on Green Bay's schedule was a visit to Baltimore on the second weekend in December. But first, the Packers faced a trip out West to meet the hapless Rams in the Coliseum. Then Minnesota was their next opponent a week later, this time at Lambeau Field. Win those two, then worry about the trip to Baltimore.

In the meantime, the Colts were spending Thanksgiving in the Motor City with the Lions. Detroit had a bad habit of knocking off visiting teams on turkey day. Lombardi went to mass that morning and asked God for a miracle, a victory by the Lions. He should have prayed a little more. The Colts and Lions tied, 24-24. The end of the game was a real tragedy. Allow me, please.

The Colts had the ball deep in their own territory with time running out on the clock. Fourth down on their own six-yard line. A punt was in order from deep in the Baltimore end zone. Into the air the ball flew, landing in the hands of Pat Studstill who had called a fair catch. The ball was placed on the Baltimore 42-yard line. Harry Gilmer, one of the dumbest head coaches in the history of football, sent his offense onto the field to run a play. The result was an incomplete pass forced by the Colts' defense. With less than 10 seconds to go in the game, Gilmer sent his placekicker, Wayne Walker, into the game to try a field goal. Walker was a better than average placekicker. He missed this one from the 49-yard line. Time runs out. Game ends. Well, a tie was better than Baltimore winning.

However, this is why Gilmer was dumber than a box of rocks. Studstill had made a fair catch. *A fair catch!* In football, even today, when you make a fair catch, you can then call for a free kick. *A free kick! Yes, a free placekick or even a punt.* The kicker picks up the ball and kicks it. Or he can have a holder put the ball on the ground to kick it. Walker could have had the ball placed on the 42-yard line, while the Colts defense stood back several yards and watched him boot the ball. If it goes through the uprights, it's three points for the Lions and they win the game, 27-24. Baltimore then would have two losses on the season, which would be a good thing for the Packers and the Bears.

But, alas! Harry Gilmer proved how smart he wasn't, and after one more season of bad decisions in Detroit, he was fired and replaced by Joe Schmidt, a Hall of Fame linebacker for the Lions.

♦♦♦

On the day of the game with the Rams, the rumor mill came up with a real doozy. According to unknown sources, Ray Nitschke was playing out his option to go free agent. This wasn't quite true. The truth was Nitschke was playing the 1965 season without a contract. If he didn't get the money he wanted, he thought Lombardi would trade him. Lombardi figured otherwise. He said, We are in the process of negotiating. He is still unsigned, but we don't feel that he is playing out his option. I think things will be straightened out."

Under NFL rules, when a player signs with another team as a free agent, his original team is given another player of equal ability or a draft choice, which is what happened in the Ron Kramer case.

Four days later Nitschke eventually received the contract he wanted all along, and he remained with the Packers for the rest of his pro career.

♦♦♦

Now for the Rams in Los Angeles.

Bill Munson, LA's second year QB, was out for the remainder of the season due to a leg injury. His back up was Roman Gabriel, the best fast-ball pitcher" in the NFL, according to Art Daley.

Herb Adderley agreed with Daley. While watching Rams game films, Adderly noticed that Gabriel stood flat-footed once and yet the ball traveled 45 yards in the air. What an arm he has!"

Gabriel faced the Packers the year before when the Rams put the kibosh on them in Milwaukee. He completed nine of 16 passes for 139 yards and one touchdown. Willie Wood and Adderly did pick off two of Gabriel's throws in that game. In his four seasons in the league, Gabriel had thrown a total of 95 passes with 50 completions for 565 yards but was intercepted five times in the five games he played against the Packers, so the LA backup QB was not invincible.

Adderly also had this to say about the West Coast team.

> ***"The Rams have a good team. They've just been hurt by bad breaks and injuries. We'll have to get off to a good start against them."***

The leader in the league with five interceptions for a total of 162 yards and two touchdowns he proved to be something of a clairvoyant—sadly.

The headline on Art Daley's story for the game with the Rams pretty much said it all.

Rams Whip Packers 21-10, Jolt Title Hopes

Daley's subhead was just as sad, if not worse.

Loss Knocks Bays 1½ Tilts Behind Colts

His opening words also struck a lot of raw nerves all across Packerland.

> ***"This one hurt … in more ways than one."***

Daley was one of the greatest sports journalists of the 20th Century. It could be said about him, He calls 'em like he sees 'em." When covering the Packers, Art seldom pulled a punch.

Once again, Daley said it like it was. The Green Bay offense came up short. All they could muster was a first quarter field goal and a final period touchdown pass from Zeke Bratkowski to Elijah Pitts who raced down field for an 80-yard score that was too late to make a difference.

In between the Pack's FG and TD, the Rams' Ben Wilson

scored their only touchdown, Bruce Gossett kicked three field goals, and Deacon Jones nailed Bratkowski in the end zone for a safety in that order to give LA a lead of 18-3. After the score by Pitts, Gossett booted his fourth three of the day to seal the victory for the Rams.

Gabriel had the game Ram fans hoped for. He connected on 15 of 28 passes for 255 yards and only one interception pulled down by Willie Wood. On the ground, the Rams rushed for 102 net yards, while the Fearsome Foursome kept the Packer run game to a meager 22 net yards. The passing game was better for the Packers, but still not good enough to make a difference in the outcome.

Coach Lombardi told the press after the game:

> ***"The tipoff on the type of game we were playing came early when we couldn't score a touchdown after recovering that fumble. When we couldn't make a first down there, I felt we were in for a rough afternoon. Sooner or later, the Rams were going to win, and it had to be us. They are much better than their record shows."***

♦♦♦

The loss to the worst team in their conference dropped the Packers to a game and a half behind the Colts with the Bears creeping up on both leaders. Chicago crunched the Giants, 35-14, in New York behind the play of rookies Gale Sayers and Dick Butkus, the Illinois blockbuster. Sayers broke the rookie record for touchdowns by scoring two and bringing his total to 14 for the year. He also gained a season best 113 yards on 13 carries. For his part, Butkus intercepted a pass, recovered a Giants fumble, and tackled every Giant he could get his hands on.

In the rest of the league, the Browns locked up the Eastern Conference title in front of their hometown fans, thumping the hapless Steelers, 42-21. In Washington, Sonny Jurgensen led the Redskins to a narrow victory over Dallas, 34-31. The Eagles nailed the Cardinals in St. Louis, 28-24. Lastly, the 49ers ripped the Vikings, 45-24.

NATIONAL FOOTBALL LEAGUE STANDINGS FOR 1965									
EASTERN CONFERENCE					WESTERN CONFERENCE				
	W	L	T	PCT.		W	L	T	PCT.
x-Cleveland	9	2	0	.818	Baltimore	9	1	1	.900
New York	5	6	0	.455	Green Bay	8	3	0	.727
St. Louis	5	6	0	.455	Chicago	7	4	0	.636
Washington	5	6	0	.455	San Francisco	6	5	0	.545
Dallas	4	7	0	.364	Detroit	5	5	1	.500
Philadelphia	4	7	0	.364	Minnesota	5	6	0	.455
Pittsburgh	2	9	0	.182	Los Angeles	2	9	0	.182

x-clinched conference

♦♦♦

The AFL posted a division winner when Boston upset Joe Namath and the Jets, 27-23, giving the Eastern crown to the idle Buffalo Bills by default. Also on Sunday, Kansas City crushed Houston, 52-21. On Thanksgiving Day, the Bills and San Diego Chargers fought to a 20-20 tie in San Diego

AMERICAN FOOTBALL LEAGUE STANDINGS FOR 1965									
EASTERN DIVISION					WESTERN DIVISION				
	W	L	T	PCT.		W	L	T	PCT.
x-Buffalo	8	2	1	.800	San Diego	6	2	3	.750
New York	4	6	1	.400	Kansas City	6	4	2	.600
Houston	4	7	0	.364	Oakland	6	4	1	.556
Boston	2	8	2	.200	Denver	4	7	0	.364

♦♦♦

On Tuesday after the Ram game, Art Daley interviewed Lombardi with all the other sports scribes from around the state of Wisconsin. The coach spoke openly as usual, and the reporters wrote down all they heard from him. Not all of what Vince said to them wound up in print or on the radio or television. But it was always good stuff for the fans across the state and the Upper Peninsula of Michigan.

> ***"I can't say we looked good, but we haven't looked any worse. I can't fault the defense,***

but the defense did not have one of its better days. The offense didn't pick up, but the passer received great protection. They got to the quarterback only once. The other time Bratkowski slipped and fell. We were overpowered in the offensive line again, and they (the Ram linemen) knocked the ball down four times."

That game on the West Coast was behind the Packers. Now they had to focus on the Vikings again.

Lombardi was really worried about playing Minnesota for the second time in three Sundays. Why? Because the Packers beat the Bears in their first meeting of the year, then lost to them in the second. Same with Detroit and Los Angeles. Beating an opponent twice in one season in the NFL is a downright tough thing to do. The Green Bay coach said an extra *Hail, Mary* at morning mass every day that week.

As usual, Art Daley told it like it is. In other words, he believed in come big or stay home." That was the theme of his Sunday story about the Packers versus the Vikings. Minnesota had nothing to play for, but the Packers had to do or die" because a loss would basically finish their season.

Apparently, all the Green Bay players, coaches, and sideline personnel read the sports section that morning of the game. When the two teams took the field, it was obvious to the crowd that the Packers were either high on some kind of drug or they were just pumped by their coach's pep talk in the locker room.

Just three plays into the game, a Minnesota running back took a solid blow from D-lineman Dave Robinson, knocking the ball loose. Herb Adderley flopped on the ball at the Vikings' 27-yard line. Bart Starr immediately called a play in the huddle, took the snap, dropped back, and hit Boyd Dowler in the end zone, giving the Packers the lead, 7-0.

The Vikings fumbled the kickoff, and Dan Grimm recovered the ball on Minnesota's 26-yard line. After gaining nine yards on two carries by Jim Taylor, Tom Moore gained nothing on third down.

But instead of having Don Chandler attempt a field goal, Lombardi chose to go for the first down. Bad luck! Starr and Moore bungled the handoff, and the Vikings recovered.

After an exchange of punts, the Vikings drove 80 yards to tie the score at 7-7. Then the Packer offense froze up for the remainder of the first quarter and much of the second. While the Pack was doing nothing, Fred Cox booted three field goals to put Minnesota ahead, 16-7. His fourth attempt fell short and right into the hands of Willie Wood who weaved his way 71 yards to the Viking 21 where he was tackled with just 19 seconds left in the half. Two plays later Elijah Pitts found the end zone from three yards out, sending the Packers into the locker room all pumped again, partially by the touchdown and partially by the two scores on the scoreboard: Vikings 16, Packers 14, and the other Bears 10, Baltimore 0.

Green Bay's defense held the Vikings to a single third quarter field goal, putting Minnesota up, 19-14. Seeing the Bears' lead over the Colts go up another field goal and Baltimore still with a goose egg, the Packers came to life again—on both sides of the line of scrimmage. The defense held the Vikings scoreless for the rest of the game, while the offense took control of the game, starting with the kickoff after the final Minnesota field goal.

Tom Moore took the ensuing kickoff and returned it 40 yards to the Green Bay 41. Then Pitts gained three yards on the first play from scrimmage. Taylor cut to his right for 16 yards and a first down on the Minnesota 40. Pitts then found an opening in the Viking line for 12 yards to the 28. After Pitts made one more yard, backup QB Zeke Bratkowski found Bill Anderson in the left flat, and the tight end steamed down the sideline for a touchdown and precarious 21-19 lead with nine seconds left in the third quarter.

Green Bay's defense then held the Vikings for three straight punts before the final score of the game was set up by a 51-yard option pass from Pitts to Carroll Dale. After a loss of five yards on three plays, Chandler booted a tipped ball just inches over the cross bar to make the final score, 24-19.

Meanwhile, the Bears completed a shutout of Baltimore, 13-0. Green Bay fans, players, coaches, and sideline personnel were more than ecstatic. They knew the game with the Colts on the following Sunday might possibly decide the conference title.

> ***"We were overrunning everything in the first half," said Vince. It was the highest I've seen my team in a long time—two or three years. They were almost too high. I thought we played a spirited game."***

For once, Lombardi was extremely succinct in his post-game media conference. Probably, he was already thinking about their next game against the Baltimore Colts who were certainly going to be more loaded for bear than they had been against Chicago.

♦♦♦

Speaking of the Colts, Baltimore lost their future Hall of Fame QB for the rest of the season, including the NFL Championship game, if the Colts were to get that far. Johnny Unitas was crunched between the two Chicago defensive tackles, Stan Jones and Earl Leggett. Backing Unitas was Gary Cuozzo, not exactly the best second-string QB in the league. The Bears made his life miserable that Sunday as they fought their way into the fight for the conference title.

Around the rest of the NFL, the 49ers came from behind in the fourth quarter with a pair of late touchdowns to squeeze a win out of the Lions, 17-14. The Rams stuck it to the Cardinals in St. Louis behind Roman Gabriel, 27-3. Cleveland continued their winning ways by dumping the Redskins, 24-16. The Giants moved into second place in the Eastern Conference with a 35-10 spanking of the Steelers. Big Jethro Pugh saved the win for the Dallas Cowboys over the Eagles in Philadelphia, 21-19. The 6-foot-7 Pugh blocked a field goal try in the third quarter, bouncing the ball all the way to the Philly 21-yard line, setting up a touchdown pass from Dandy Don Meredith to Frank Clark in the end zone for what proved to be the winning TD.

NATIONAL FOOTBALL LEAGUE STANDINGS FOR 1965									
EASTERN CONFERENCE					WESTERN CONFERENCE				
	W	L	T	PCT.		W	L	T	PCT.
x-Cleveland	10	2	0	.833	Baltimore	9	2	1	.818
New York	6	6	0	.500	Green Bay	9	3	0	.750
St. Louis	5	7	0	.417	Chicago	8	4	0	.667
Washington	5	7	0	.417	San Francisco	7	5	0	.583
Dallas	5	7	0	.417	Detroit	5	6	1	.455
Philadelphia	4	8	0	.333	Minnesota	5	7	0	.417
Pittsburgh	2	10	0	.167	Los Angeles	3	9	0	.250

x-clinched conference

♦♦♦

On Saturday, John Hadl led the San Diego Chargers to a 38-7 victory over the New York Jets in San Diego, bringing the Chargers only one game away from claiming the division title. Then on Sunday, Oakland beat Denver, 24-13, and Buffalo hammered Houston, 29-18. Boston and Kansas City had the week off.

AMERICAN FOOTBALL LEAGUE STANDINGS FOR 1965									
EASTERN DIVISION					WESTERN DIVISION				
	W	L	T	PCT.		W	L	T	PCT.
x-Buffalo	9	2	1	.818	San Diego	7	2	3	.778
New York	4	7	1	.364	Oakland	7	4	1	.636
Houston	4	8	0	.333	Kansas City	6	4	2	.600
Boston	2	8	2	.200	Denver	4	8	0	.333

x-clinched division

♦♦♦

One big question faced the Packer brain trust in the days before the ***HUGE*** game with the Colts in Baltimore. How would the Ponies react to the loss of their leader and future Hall of Fame quarterback?

Coach Lombardi voiced his thoughts on that uncertainty to the press on Tuesday before practice.

> ***"A lot of teams will become aroused and play better with a key player out. We had a similar***

situation a few years ago and won three out of four games."

He was referring to the loss of Bart Starr who broke his hand in 1963 and the way the team rallied around his replacement John Roach.

Lombardi added another thought: the crowd.

"They gave (Rudy) Bukich (Bears QB) a hard time out there last Sunday with their screaming and yelling. I don't think he could hear a thing. You can bet the crowd will have the Colts aroused."

That sentiment was supported by another voice, this one from a hospital in Baltimore.

"They (Colts) can do it if they make up their minds."

The speaker was none other than Johnny Unitas, Baltimore coach Don Shula said the Colts could win without their great quarterback.

"We'll have a full week to get Gary Cuozzo ready. He will be working with the No. 1 receivers all week, and I think he'll be ready."

While he was with the Packers in Maryland, Art Daley came up with eight different scenarios for the NFL's Western Conference last two weeks of games to be played by the only three teams left in the running. Those teams were Baltimore, Chicago, and Green Bay. Only one had the Packers winning the title outright by winning their last two regular season games. In the others, he had the Packers in ties for the crown. Two with Baltimore and one with the Bears. He even had one where the Monsters of the Midway would win the conference outright. The other three outcomes had the Colts winning and meeting the Browns in the NFL Championship Game on January 2.

Lombardi told his players to ignore Daley's column and focus on winning the game in Baltimore on Sunday and think of nothing else. His guys got the message.

Baltimore scored first on a Lou Michaels field goal from 14 yards out. The Packers then drove down the field to the two-yard line. At that point, Paul Hornung put Green Bay ahead with a burst into the end zone. Don Chandler added the PAT to put the Pack ahead, 7-3. From that point on, the Pack held the lead. Six minutes later Hornung caught a pass from Bart Starr and raced 51 yards for his second TD of the day.

The Colts retaliated with another field goal and Lenny Moore TD from two yards out to bring Baltimore close at 14-13. Boyd Dowler then caught a Starr pass for a 10-yard touchdown and Chandler extra point. That made the halftime score, 21-13.

In the second half, the Packers defense shut the door on the Colts first possession, with Willie Davis, Ron Kostelnik, and Lionel Aldridge each making tackles for losses and a total of minus 13 yards. The punt those D-linemen forced on Baltimore was reeled in by Willie Wood at the Colts' 40. From there, Taylor bolted for 10 yards, Starr connected with Max McGee for 14 yards, and Hornung scored his second TD on a nine-yard sweep around left end for his third TD of the day and putting the Packers farther ahead, 28-13. The Golden Boy was smashed into the first base wall by a Colt defender. Hornung was hurt on the play but not enough to keep him out of the game.

On the Colts' next drive, Tom Brown intercepted a Tom Matte pass to set up the Packers on their own 45. In 11 plays, Starr connected on passes to Dowler and Taylor for 17 yards and 10 yards, respectively. Taylor also had an 11-yard run, and Hornung capped the drive with a three-yard burst into the end zone for his fourth touchdown of the day.

Baltimore scored twice to make the score, 35-27. Unfazed by the Colts' rally, Starr fired a bullet down the middle to Hornung who then raced the distance to the end zone. The play covered 65 yards and put Hornung's fifth TD on the board, giving the Packers a solid lead, 42-27, with 4:22 left on the clock.

The Colts wouldn't give up until Bob Jeter intercepted another Baltimore pass to halt the drive. Green Bay ran off some more clock, then punted on fourth down with the ball on the home team's 34. The game ended in favor of the Packers, 42-27, but more important, those boys from the little town in Wisconsin were once again in first place in the Western Conference.

On the day, Taylor gained 66 yards on 17 carries, Hornung marked 61 yards on 15 carries to go along with his record-tying five touchdowns. The kid from Notre Dame also snared two passes for 115 yards to give him a total of 176 yards offensively. Taylor caught two passes for 39 yards to make his total offense for the contest 105 yards.

♦♦♦

Eastern Conference champion Cleveland traveled to California in Week 13 and were smoked by the Rams, 42-7. Superstar Jim Brown said after the game,

> ***"It would be unrealistic to say we played like we did when we were playing for the championship. Mud is mud. The main trouble was their defense, not the mud."***

The weather was far from being the best for playing football.

In other games, the Bears remained in contention with a 61-0 blistering of the 49ers in Chicago. Rising superstar Gale Sayers tied the NFL record of six TDs in a game set initially by Ernie Nevers of the Chicago Cardinals in 1929 and tied by Dub Jones of Cleveland in 1951. Sayers also rushed for 113 yards, caught passes for 89 yards, and ran back punts 134 yards for a total 326 yards on the day, the second most in a game since Wally Triplet of Detroit set the mark at 331 against the Los Angeles in 1950.

Other scores around the NFL were Dallas 27, St. Louis 13 on Saturday night. New York trounced Washington, 27-10. Philadelphia stomped on Pittsburgh, 47-13. Minnesota kicked the stuffing out of a hapless Detroit, 29-7.

NATIONAL FOOTBALL LEAGUE STANDINGS FOR 1965									
EASTERN CONFERENCE					WESTERN CONFERENCE				
	W	L	T	PCT.		W	L	T	PCT.
x-Cleveland	10	3	0	.769	Green Bay	10	3	0	.769
New York	7	6	0	.538	Baltimore	9	3	1	.750
Dallas	6	7	0	.462	Chicago	9	4	0	.692
Philadelphia	5	8	0	.385	San Francisco	7	6	0	.538
St. Louis	5	8	0	.385	Minnesota	6	7	0	.462
Washington	5	8	0	.385	Detroit	5	7	1	.417
Pittsburgh	2	11	0	.154	Los Angeles	4	9	0	.308

x-clinched conference

♦♦♦

The AFL races for the division titles were settled on Sunday when the San Diego Chargers trimmed the Houston Oilers, 37-26. Buffalo's Bills continued their winning ways with a 34-25 victory over Kansas City. The Oakland Raiders guaranteed themselves a 2nd place finish with a 24-14 over the New York Jets. Boston made their final game of the year meaningful by dumping Denver, 28-20.

AMERICAN FOOTBALL LEAGUE STANDINGS FOR 1965									
EASTERN DIVISION					WESTERN DIVISION				
	W	L	T	PCT.		W	L	T	PCT.
x-Buffalo	10	2	1	.833	San Diego	8	2	3	.800
New York	4	8	1	.333	Oakland	8	4	1	.667
Houston	4	9	0	.308	Kansas City	6	5	2	.545
Boston	3	8	2	.273	Denver	4	9	0	.308

x-clinched division

♦♦♦

All the Packers had to do to win the Western Conference title was to beat the 49ers in San Francisco in the last game of the regular season. Then they could play host to the Cleveland Browns at Lambeau Field. Piece of cake, right?

The Packers held down the 49ers, 27-10, when the two teams squared off in Lambeau Field back in October. This game was played a week after the Gold Rushers had been in Baltimore and lost a tough one, 27-24. The Golden Gaters were pretty beat up after playing the Colts in their first go-around. When the Ponies went west to face those pesky 49ers in Kezar Stadium, their second meeting was played much like the first one. San Francisco got a lead, then Johnny Unitas led his team to a 34-28 victory.

More to the point, would the 49ers play like they did when they faced the Bears in Frisco to open the season? Or would they be like the team that faced the Monsters of the Midway in Week 13? The 49ers handled the Bears in Frisco, 52-24, then were totally embarrassed by a rookie running back and his teammates, 61-20. Packer fans had their hopes pinned on the latter meeting of the two teams in Wrigley Field.

Not so Coach Lombardi and his staff. They knew the 49ers were a tough team, especially on their home field. Besides beating the Bears in Frisco, the 49ers had beaten Pittsburgh, Los Angeles, and Detroit at Kezar Stadium. Their two losses at home were against Minnesota, 42-41, and Baltimore, 27-24. Either one or both of those games could have gone the other way. If the 49ers had pulled those two games out of their back pockets, then San Francisco would have a record of 9-4 and be tied with the Bears for second place. Better than that, Baltimore would be out of the race for conference title with a record of 8-4-1. That tie game the Colts had with the Lions would have dropped them out of the race.

B-b-u-u-t-t-t! That wasn't the way it was. The Packers had a record of 10-3 and were a half game ahead of the Colts. A victory over San Francisco would put the Pack into the NFL Championship Game against the well-rested Cleveland Browns.

S-s-s-o-o-o! Beating Frisco? Sounded easy enough, but was it?

Art Daley wrote in the *Press-Gazette*,

> ***"The biggest problem with the 49ers is containing their offense, which is the 'yardiest' and highest scoring in the league."***

Green Bay's biggest headache was Frisco's quarterback John Brodie, who had completed 60.5 per cent of his passes, but he also had thrown 13 interceptions, five more than Bart Starr, whose completion rate was 57.0. The biggest pain in the rump was 49ers' running back Ken Willard, who was fourth highest in yards gained with 769. He was also the seventh best rusher for average at 4.1 per carry.

Those numbers meant the Packers defensive line had to stop Willard and corral Brodie, while the Green Bay secondary had to put a lid on Frisco's receivers, especially Dave Parks, the number one pass catcher in the league with 71 catches, 1,195 yards gained, and 11 TDs.

Finally, the Packers had to do something about Tommy Davis, the top placekicker in the NFL with 49 PATs in 50 tries.

On the other side of the line, Frisco was rather poor at keeping their opponents off the scoreboard. Pittsburgh and Detroit were the only two teams to score fewer than 21 points against the 49ers. For the season, San Francisco gave up an average of just over 29 points per game.

Lombardi knew all those numbers before he put his team on the field in Kezar Stadium. He also knew Jim Taylor was still suffering with a groin pull that had hampered him during the Baltimore game. The coach described Taylor as doubtful for the game with the 49ers. His spot was being run in practice by Tom Moore and rookie Allen Jacobs. Without Taylor, the Packers running game might have been suspect. Paul Hornung thought otherwise. He expressed more of his opinion the day before the game.

"I just know he'll be ready for the game."

That night the Packers learned that Baltimore had pulled out a close win in Los Angeles, 20-17. The Rams led, 14-10, going into the final quarter. Newly acquired quarterback Ed Brown, veteran of 12 years in the NFL with the Bears for eight of those years and four with the Steelers and this one game for the Colts, entered the game late. He connected on a 68-yard pass play to future Hall of Famer John Mackey to tie the game. Then Lou Michaels booted the winning field goal from 23 yards out late in the game. Roman Gabriel didn't give up. He passed and ran his team down field from their own 33 to the Baltimore seven. A field goal would have tied the game, but a touchdown would win it. Then with 1:07 left in the game, Gabriel did the unthinkable. He threw an interception to Baltimore defensive back Bob Boyd. The Colts then ran out the clock and put a ton of pressure on the Packers to beat the 49ers on Sunday.

♦♦♦

In games of little importance except for players' egos, Cleveland shut down St. Louis, 27-24. Dallas dumped New York, 38-20, to earn the right to play the loser of the Packers-Colts title game in the Playoff Bowl in Miami. Washington put Pittsburgh out of their misery, 35-14. Detroit bounced Philadelphia, 35-28. And the Bears lost to Minnesota, 24-17, despite Gale Sayers setting a new record for touchdowns with 22 on the year.

NATIONAL FOOTBALL LEAGUE STANDINGS FOR 1965									
EASTERN CONFERENCE					WESTERN CONFERENCE				
	W	L	T	PCT.		W	L	T	PCT.
x-Cleveland	11	3	0	.769	*Baltimore	10	3	1	.769
Dallas	7	7	0	.500	*Green Bay	10	3	1	.769
New York	7	7	0	.500	Chicago	9	5	0	.643
Washington	6	8	0	.429	San Francisco	7	6	1	.538
Philadelphia	5	9	0	.357	Minnesota	7	7	0	.500
St. Louis	5	9	0	.357	Detroit	6	7	1	.462
Pittsburgh	2	12	0	.143	Los Angeles	4	10	0	.286

x-clinched conference*-Tied for Conference Title

♦♦♦

Although the division titles were settled the previous week, the AFL still had games to play. On Saturday, Boston beat the pants off the Houston Oilers, 42-14. For Sunday games, Buffalo lost to AFL Rookie of the Year Joe Namath and the New York Jets, 14-12. San Diego took down Oakland, 24-14. And Kansas City dumped Denver, 45-35. While the Packers and Colts were deciding who would face the Browns for the NFL crown, San Diego would be hosting Buffalo for the 5th AFL championship.

AMERICAN FOOTBALL LEAGUE STANDINGS FOR 1965									
EASTERN DIVISION					WESTERN DIVISION				
	W	L	T	PCT.		W	L	T	PCT.
x-Buffalo	10	3	1	.769	x-San Diego	9	2	3	.818
New York	5	8	1	.385	Oakland	8	5	1	.615
Boston	4	8	2	.333	Kansas City	7	5	2	.583
Housto n	4	10	0	.286	Denver	4	10	0	.286

x-clinched division

♦♦♦

All the Packers had to do to win the Western Conference title was beat San Francisco.

The Sabbath arrived. Lombardi prayed. Then the game.

If the Packers won, they would tackle the Browns for the NFL championship. If they lost, they would play the Cowboys in the Playoff Bowl in Miami. A tie with San Francisco would result in a playoff game with Colts—***IN LAMBEAU FIELD.***

The 49ers got off to a 3-0 lead with 2:21 gone in the second quarter, but the Pack charged back with a touchdown, a 43-yard pass play from Bart Starr to Boyd Dowler and a PAT by Don Chandler, to go up 7-3 at the half.

Nine minutes into the third quarter, Herb Adderley stole a pass on the Frisco 11 and returned it for a TD, moving the Green Bay lead up to 14-3. Then Brodie went to work again, connecting with John David Crow on a 32-yard pass play with 3:57 left in the third period.

Four minutes and 22 seconds into the final period, Brodie found Parks in the end zone from 11 yards out to give the 49ers the lead, 17-14. Four minutes and 20 seconds after that, Jim Taylor crashed through the line and into the end zone for six points. Chandler added the PAT, and Packers had the lead again, 21-17. On their next drive, the Green Bay offense stalled on the San Francisco 24-yard line. The sideline boss called for a field goal try, and Chandler came through to put the lead up seven points at 24-17.

With only two minutes to go in the game, Brodie went to work again, starting on his own 44. Not because the kickoff return was done, but because a Packer defender had been called for a face mask penalty. Brodie hit Parks for 12 yards, Gary Lewis for seven, Parks again for nine, and tight end Vern Burke 27 yards and a TD. Davis converted the PAT, and the game was tied at 24 points for each team.

The Packers still had a minute seven seconds left to get into field goal range. Starting on their own 32, Starr quickly got a first down on the 42 with 52 seconds left. Then three Starr passes went awry. With fourth down and 10 to go, Lombardi had no choice but to call for a punt in order to protect the tie.

Chandler booted the ball, and Kermit Alexander received it on the Frisco 16 and weaved his way 38 yards to the Green Bay 46 with seven seconds still on the clock. Instead of going for a 53-yard field goal, San Francisco coach Jack Christian called for one more play. Brodie threw a quicky to the left, but the ball went out of bounds. The

49er field goal team started onto the field, but an official signaled the game was over.

San Francisco fans and their team all screamed bloody murder. However, the timekeeper felt otherwise. Final score? 24-24.

The Packers had a tie, and their record for the season matched that of Baltimore. Both teams finished the regular season with records of 10-3-1.

A tie for first place in the regular season meant the two teams had to play one game for the crown.

To Baltimore's chagrin, the playoff game would be played at Lambeau Field in Green Bay by virtue of the Packers winning the coin flip by the commissioner.

Green Bay fans were ecstatic!

§ § §

10

Playoff for the Conference Title

Just one more game to go to settle the right to play the Cleveland Browns on their own field. The Packers were within two minutes of their fourth Western Conference title in six years, but they fell short and wound up with a tie.

Now the Packers were 60 minutes removed from the National Football League Championship game. All they had to do was defeat the Baltimore Colts—for the third time in 1965.

Defeating any team in almost any sport three times in a row in a single season is statistically hard to do. Two out of three? Happens all the time in professional sports. Two out of three in a baseball home stand? A mathematical certainty. Winning all three? Ask any manager of any team, and he'll chuckle a bit then tell you he'd take two of three anytime.

Lombardi noted one of the many ways to measure the coming playoff game. This is the greatest publicity for the City of Green Bay." The Baltimore-Green Bay game would be on nationwide television until the AFL championship game telecast would start at three o'clock that same afternoon.

But this wasn't all that was of big importance to Green Bay *and* Wisconsin. If the Packers were to win the playoff game, they would be Western Conference champions and would be on national TV again the following week because the NFL Championship game would be played in Lambeau Field.

Meanwhile, the Colts were prepping for the playoff game with hopes of winning and getting a chance to avenge themselves on the Browns who had beaten them the year before in the Championship contest. The two quarterbacks, Ed Brown and George Haffner, were declared ineligible for the playoff game by the

NFL owners.

Of course, the Baltimore coaching staff's desires were shaky at best because they had no real quarterback. Well, they did have one or two. Halfback Tom Matte and corner back Bobby Boyd.

Matte had been a quarterback at Ohio State under Woody Hayes, the legendary coach who declared,

"Three things can happen when you throw a pass, and two of them are bad."

Hayes seldom called for his quarterbacks to throw the ball. Matte did throw many passes, especially long ones to receivers running at a gallop. Under Hs, he ran the ball more often than he passed it.

Boyd played quarterback, defensive back, and punt returner at Oklahoma under the great Bud Wilkinson, who still holds the record for the longest winning streak by an NCAA Division 1 team, a streak started after a defeat by Notre Dame in 1953 and ended by Notre Dame four years later in 1957 after 47 consecutive wins.* Like Hayes, Wilkinson didn't use the forward pass very much. Thus, Boyd seldom threw a pass in college.

In the game against the Rams, Matte had done a relatively good job at quarterback, but the man who led the Colts to victory in the final minutes was former Bear Ed Brown. Had Baltimore not had Brown available, there would have been no playoff game with Green Bay.*

But the playoff game was on.

Baltimore coach Don Shula worked both Matte and Boyd for the game with the Packers. Matte said,

"At least I know where I stand now … all alone. But I can't have any more pressure on me than I had last week, so what difference does it make? I guess the pressure will be on Bobby Boyd. He'll have to learn what to Matte would be wearing a plastic band on his left forearm. Inside the band was a list of plays for him to call should he fail to read Coach Shula's signals from the sidelines.

If I'm grasping for something to do, I can take a peek," said Matte. Even if the Packers see the list, it won't help them. They already know our plays but they still have to guess which one is coming next."

During the middle of the week, the *Associated Press* sportswriters published their NFL All-Pro list. Four Packers made the first team, three on defense and one on offense.

The lone offensive All-Pro was none other than Forrest Gregg, the man who could play either tackle spot or either guard position. He was selected as a guard.

♦♦♦

Willie Davis was named to the first team as a defensive end. Joining him on the first team were Herb Adderley as a corner back and Willie Wood as a safety. Ray Nitschke was selected to the second team.

Edging Nitschke out of the voting, was Chicago's rookie monster linebacker Dick Butkus. The only other rookie to make the first team was Gale Sayers, also a member of the Midway Monsters.

♦♦♦

Statistically, the Colts. bettered the Packers in almost every category. *Almost!* Some stats were more important than others, and it was those lesser numbers that mostly favored Green Bay.

OFFENSE
First Downs: **Colts 266**, Pack 201
Total Yards: **Colts 4,598**, Pack 3,601
Rushing Yards: **Colts 1,593**, Pack 1,488
Net Passing Yards: **Colts 3,005**, Pack 2,113
Net Passes Attempted: Colts 399, **Pack 305**
Passes Completed: **Colts 222**, Pack 166
Per Cent Passes Completed: **Colts 55.6**, Pack 54.4
Yards Gained Passing: **Colts 3,330**, Pack 2,508
Sacks/Yards Sacked: **Colts 43/325**, Pack 43/395

Passes Had Intercepted: Colts 17, **Pack 14**
OFFENSE CON'T
Yards Opponent Returned Interceptions: Colts 341, **Pack 209**
Opponent TDs Returning Interceptions: Colts 1, Pack 1
Total Punts: **Colts 56**, Pack 74
Average Yards per Punt: Colts 39.6, **Pack 42.9**
Punts Returned: **Colts 45**, Pack 22
Average Yards per Return: **Colts 9.4**, Pack 3.0
Kickoffs Returned: **Colts 52**, Pack 50
Average Yards per Return: **Colts 23.9**, Pack 20.8
Penalties: Colts 69, **Pack 48**
Yards Penalized: Colts 616, **Pack 529**
Opponents Fumbles Recovered: Colts 14, **Pack 23**
Touchdowns: **Colts 48**, Pack 38
TDs Running: Colts 17, **Pack 19**
TDs Passing: **Colts 31**, Pack 19
PATs: **Colts 48**, Pack 37
FGs: Colts 17, Pack 17
FGs Attempted: Colts 26, Pack 26
Total Points: **Colts 389**, Pack 316
DEFENSE
Opponents Points: Colts 284, **Pack 224**
Opponents First Downs: **Colts 233**, Pack 240
Rushing First Downs: **Colts 78**, Pack 115
Passing First Downs: Colts 131, **Pack 111**
Penalties: Colts 24, **Pack 14**
Opponents Yards Gained: Colts 4,045, **Pack 3,969**
Net Rushing Yards Allowed: **Colts 1,483**, Pack 1,988
Net Passing Yards Allowed: Colts 2,562, **Pack 1,981**
Opponents Rushing Attempts: Colts 410, **Pack 480**
Average Yards Allowed per Rushing Attempt: **Colts 3.8**, Pack 4.1
Opponents Pass Attempts: **Colts 400**, Pack 383
Opponents Pass Completions: Colts 213, **Pack 187**
Per Cent Passes Completed: Colts 53.3, **Pack 48.8**
Opponents Passes Intercepted: Colts 22, **Pack 27**
Return Yards Intercepted Passes: Colts 318, **Pack 561**

Returns for Touchdowns: Colts 4, Pack 4
DEFENSE CON'T
Opponents Punt Returned: Colts 26, **Pack 36**
Average Yards per Return: Colts 7.6, **Pack 8.1**
Opponents Kickoff Returns: Colts 63, **Pack 52**
Average Yards per Kickoff Return: Colts 21.4, **Pack 23.4**
Opponents Touchdowns: Colts 35, **Pack 22**
Opponents Rushing Touchdowns: Colts 13, **Pack 11**
Opponents Passing Touchdowns: Colts 22, **Pack 11**

Now these are not all the categories that were published in the *Press-Gazette*. This author selected those that were most important to show the difference between the Colts' and Packers' regular seasons.

Baltimore was a team that lived and died by the forward pass, while Green Bay relied on ball control and *defense in all phases of the game.*

Lombardi knew and believed in that adage that football games are won—or lost—in the trenches. From his very start as head coach of the Green Bay Packers, he built his team around his offensive line as well as defensive line.

Every running back and quarterback worth his salt will say they are only as good as the men blocking for them. On the other side of the line, the down linemen must be strong and agile afoot. Linebackers must recognize in the wink of an eye where the holes in the line are and how to attack through them.

Vince Lombardi built his teams on these principles. The stats for every season he coached proved this to be so. The 1965 campaign was a prime example. So sayeth the statistics of the Colts and the Pack.

Of offensive numbers, the Packers had only seven categories where they bettered the Colts. Whereas, the Colts had 17 with four either tied or insignificant. Thus, the Colts were the better offensive team by 10 categories.

Of defensive numbers, the Packers had 16 categories where they bettered the Colts, and Baltimore had only a mere four with three either insignificant or tied. Thus, Green Bay was the better team on defense by a solid dozen categories, besting the Colts by two categories overall. In other words, statistically the Packers were the better team and should be the favorite come Sunday in Lambeau Field.

Lombardi brought up the intangible category at Wednesday's press conference.

> ***"Psychologically, the Colts have something going for them," he said, referring to Baltimore's 20-17 win over the Rams and the Green Bay's tie with San Francisco the previous Sunday. They've been reprieved. They've got to think they're reprieved. This has got to give them, psychologically at least, a little bit of an edge."***

He went on to compare the Colts.' loss of both of their quarterbacks to the Packer championship game of 1962, where Green Bay had suffered a lot of injuries late in the season.

> ***"Adversity made that club a better team, but in war and in football the teams with the guns are usually the winners."***

The Packers were favored to win by a touchdown. At game time, the temperature at Lambeau Field a was balmy 28 degrees. Balmy for Wisconsin in the last week of December. The Colts kicked off.

On the very first play, Bart Starr tossed a short pass 11 yards to Billy Anderson who caught it, took a few steps, got blasted by a rocket named Lenny Lyles, and fumbled the ball. Baltimore linebacker Don Shinnick scooped up the ball at the GB 25-yard line and raced into the Pack's end zone, a mere 21 seconds into the game. Lou Michaels converted the PAT, and the Colts had the lead, 7-0.

To make matters worse for the Packers, Starr headed toward Shinnick but failed to get to him because safety Jim Welch rammed him in the ribcage. The injury was so bad Starr sat out the game the remainder of the day. Into the battle came Zeke Bratkowski

After the next kickoff, Bratkowski led the offense to a pair of first downs. Then another mishap by the offense occurred. Halfback Paul Hornung fumbled at midfield. Quickstep Lyles jumped on this miscue, setting up the Baltimore offense for a short drive to the Pack end zone.

On their very first play from scrimmage, Lenny Moore takes a handoff from Tom Matte, moves ahead a few feet, and gets whomped by Packer defenders end Willie Davis and cornerback Herb Adderley at the same time. Moore loses the ball, and GB defensive back Tom Brown pounces on the ball at the midfield line.

The Packers run three plays only to come up short of a first down just inside the 40-yard line. Lombardi sends Don Chandler into the game to try a field goal from the 47. Unfortunately, the kick goes wide. The score remains, 7-0.

Both teams possess the ball three times each, and both teams kick punts three times each as the clock moves midway into the second quarter. Then the Colts., with the help of a Packer roughing the passer penalty, piece together four first downs to the Green Bay 15. Their drive is finally stalled by the Packers defense at the GB seven. Coach Don Shula sends Michaels into the game to kick a field goal. A clean hold, and Michaels makes good. The Baltimore lead increases to 10-0.

The Packers hammered back with two first downs, chiefly on passes from Bratkowski to Carroll Dale and Paul Hornung. Bob Long was racing to the end zone to catch a bomb by Bratkowski when he was grabbed by Baltimore safety Jim Welch at the nine-yard line. The Packers seemed a cinch to score, especially when Anderson caught a pass on the one-yard line. On second down, Jim Taylor was held for no gain. Hornung then took a shot at scoring on third down but only came up inches from the goal line. Next play Bratkowski handed off to Taylor again. Trying the right side of the line, Jim T was crunched by Michaels and Welch who make him fumble. Taylor recovered the ball … within a foot of the goal line.

So ends the first half.

The second half begins with the Packers kicking to

Baltimore.. After the Colts make a first down, the Green Bay defense forces a punt by Tom Gilburg. Center Buzz Nutter hikes the ball too high, forcing his kicker to jump to catch it. Gilburg has no chance to boot the ball and is tackled by Lee Roy Caffey and Bob Jeter on the Baltimore 35. Packers ball.

On second down, Carroll Dale makes a diving catch of a Zeke Bratkowski pass at the four-yard line. The agile receiver slides toward the goal line but comes up short, officially the one-yard line. Two plays later Hornung slams his way into the end zone. Chandler converts to make the score Baltimore 10, Green Bay 7.

After another Gilburg punt, the Packers started to move the ball again with Bratkowski passing to Hornung for 19 and Anderson for seven to midfield. Then another miscue. A pass to Dale was picked off by Bobby Boyd. Green Bay's defense held again, and Gilburg put a foot to the ball again. Again, the Packers offense got practically nowhere in three plays. End of the third quarter.

With fourth and a yard to go on the first play of the final stanza, Lombardi sent Chandler in to punt. He kicked the ball, but the Colts were offside, giving the boys in green and gold the ball again on the Baltimore 49. Bratkowski hit Dowler for seven and Hornung for 10. Then Hornung and Taylor clipped the Colts for 11 yards and a first down on the visitor's 21. The drive ended when Bratkowski's pass to Dowler was ripped away by Baltimore safety Jerry Logan who returned the ball 12 yards to his team's 20.

With time starting to become a serious factor in the game, the Colts punter booted another kick, putting the Pack on their own 28. This time the offense held onto the ball for 14 plays to the Colts 15. Bratkowski hit short passes to Dowler, Hornung, and Anderson Zeke for 15 yards. Taylor and Tom Moore gained a few yards but not enough for a first down. Lombardi sent Chandler into the game, and the Packers placekicker put the ball through the uprights from 22 yards out to tie the game at 10-all. Gilburg was forced to punt again. The Packers had only 27 seconds left in regulation. They could only get to the Baltimore 46 before time expired.

Overtime.

The Packers won the coin toss and took the ball.

Both teams went three out. On their second possession, the

Packers went backward, and Chandler had to punt. Colts ball on their own 41. Matte ran for 14 yards in two carries up the middle to the GB 45. The Baltimore QB ripped off another eight yards before the defense stopped the Colts for two one-yard losses. Michaels tried a field goal but missed.

Green Bay ball. Baltimore Colts were worn out. The Packers drove 10 plays down to the visitors 18. Fourth down. Chandler entered the game for the final time on this day. He connected from the 25 for the winning points, 13-10.

The kick that tied the score was close to missing. Some men of the press up in their perch on the west side of the stadium said the ball failed to go through the uprights. Two Baltimore players said Chandler missed by three feet. Even one of the gents calling the game for radio and television said Chandler missed by inches. To their chagrin, the two referees standing under the goal posts called the kick, and both threw their arms straight up, signaling the field goal was GOOD!

The Packers were set to live another day.

Bring on the Browns!

§ § §

11

Cleveland vs. Green Bay - For the Win

Head coach of the Cleveland Browns Blanton Collier had been rooting for the Colts to beat the Packers in the Western Conference playoff game. Why? Simple. Baltimore didn't have a real quarterback, and that would give his team a real advantage over the Colts in the National Football League Championship Game.

Instead, the Packers would be the Browns opponent in the NFL Championship, and Green Bay would not only have one true QB in the big bout. The Packers would have two or even three, if the injury Bart Starr suffered in the very first seconds of the playoff game with Baltimore healed by Sunday's kickoff in Lambeau Field.

When he was asked how the Packers looked, Collier replied,

> ***"Their defense is something like that of the Dallas Cowboys. I'd say their offense resembles that of St. Louis, the one the Cardinals had before injuries hit the team."***

Collier meant he thought the Packers were tough both ways. To him, Dallas had the stingiest defense in the Eastern Conference. As for the offense, he meant the 49-13 beating his team took from the Cardinals early in the season before they piled up all those injuries that made them a mediocre squad much of the remaining season.

Collier was asked several more questions in the interview prior to leaving Cleveland for the NFL Championship game in Green Bay.

Question: Were you impressed with the Green Bay

linebackers against the Baltimore Colts?

> Answer: ***I certainly was. I guess Ray Nitschke must be the top middle linebacker in the league. Their three regulars all have an unusual combination of height, weight, and speed."***
>
> Q. How about the defensive line?
>
> ***A. This is a different type of defensive line from overpowering ones like those of Detroit and Los Angeles. Fellows like Henry Jordan and Willie Davis use that quickness and mobility to get the job done. Lionel Aldridge and Ron Kostelnik are more the conventional, big, strong types."***

Q. How did Paul Hornung and Jim Taylor look to you against Baltimore on Sunday?

> ***A: Too good. Hornung seemed to be running as well as ever. Taylor is the type of player who scratches and squirms for every yard. He works well in close quarters. If there's any running room, he usually finds it."***

Q. Will Cleveland's game plans be changed if Zeke Bratkowski is the quarterback rather than Bart Starr?

> ***A: We'll do just about the same things against either of them. I have a high regard for Starr. He has talent plus ability to follow a game plan. I believe he's been bothered by sore ribs much of this year. It may have hampered his throwing. As a result, Bratkowski has played quite a bit."***

Green Bay's biggest threat was fullback Jim Brown, the

greatest runner in NFL history. He started every game of every year during his entire nine-year career. His rushing yards average of 104.3 per game is still the all-time high. He was selected to the Pro Bowl every year of his career. In his final season, he averaged 110.3 yards per game for a total of 1,544 yards with 17 touchdowns rushing and four receiving passes, a total of 21 that was only beaten by Gale Sayers who had 22 for the Chicago Bears.

Middle linebacker Ray Nitschke had the honor of putting the brakes on Brown for the Packers. Unfortunately, the NFL statisticians of Nitschke's era didn't keep track of tackles made, but if they had, Ray would have been in the top 10 for his 15-year career.

Historically, in regular season and post-season games, Green Bay and Cleveland were even at three wins each. The Browns led in the regular season, three games to two, while the Packers won their only post-season match with the Browns in the Playoff Bowl of 1964 in Miami.

Finally, game day arrived. So did frigid temperatures and four inches of snow. Even so, this was football, and the game must go on, unless, of course, lightning bolts struck. Fortunately, no electricity from the sky appeared that day except that from the noisiest crowd in Lambeau Field's history. Packer fans were ecstatic through the entire game.

Green Bay won the coin toss, and Cleveland chose to kick off from the south end of the field. Lou The Toe" Groza kicked off to Tom Moore who returned the ball from the goal line to the 23-yard line. Paul Hornung took the first hand off from a healthy Bart Starr, and the Golden Boy picked up three yards. Starr's first pass fell incomplete. His second went to Jim Taylor over the middle for 10 yards and a first down.

Taylor bulldozed his way through the Cleveland line for three yards. Starr passed to Hornung for eight yards and another first down on the Green Bay 47. Fans went wild to see their favorite quarterback back in action and already two out of three passing.

Taylor took the next handoff from Starr and charged up the middle for six yards. Starr passed to Carroll Dale on the left sideline 13 yards from the goal line and pranced into the end zone when the man defending him slipped and fell down. With 11:08 remaining, the

Pack had a 7-0 lead.

Chandler kicked off, and the Cleveland receiver returned it 14 yards to the 34. Quarterback Frank Ryan threw to Jim Brown 30 yards down to the Green Bay 36. Next play Ryan found Paul Warfield for 19 yards and another first down. Staying with the air attack, Ryan found Gary Collins in the right corner end zone. A bad snap foiled Groza's PAT attempt, and the Packers kept the lead, 7-6.

Groza kicked off into the end zone, and the Packers downed it, taking the ball to their own 20. Hornung carried first and lost a yard. Starr's next pass fell incomplete. Making matters worse, trying another pass, Starr was sacked on Green Bay's 11. Don Chandler punted to Leroy Kelly who called for a fair catch on the Pack's 39.

Cleveland picked up a first down at the Green Bay 25. Brown was stopped by Willie Davis after a five-yard gain. Ryan faded to pass, ran to the right, and gained three yards. After Ryan's next pass hit the ground incomplete, Groza booted a field goal to put the Browns on top, 9-7.

The Toe" kicked off to Tom Brown who received the ball on the three and returned it to the Green Bay 24. Taylor lost two yards, then Starr's pass landed on the turf, but a holding penalty by Cleveland gave the Pack a first down on their own 27. On first down, Hornung followed Taylor around the left side for a nice gain of 34 yards to the Cleveland 39. Starr then connected with Boyd Dowler for 11 yards and another first down on the Browns' 28. Taylor burst through the left side for seven yards. He picked up another four yards and a first down on the next play. Hornung gained four, Taylor picked up four, and Hornung swept three yards through the left side and a first down as the quarter came to an end.

With the ball on Cleveland's six-yard line, Taylor plunged up the middle for three yards. Hornung tried the left side again, but the Browns were wise to him, holding him for no gain. Starr dropped back to pass, but two Cleveland attackers nailed him for five-yard loss. In came the kicking team, and Chandler split the uprights for three points and set the lead at 10-9 for the Packers.

Chandler kicked off into the end zone, and the Browns started their next pass on their own 20. Brown made three yards on first down. Ernie Green followed with five yards. Ryan handed off to Brown on third down, but Lee Roy Caffey stopped Big Jim dead in his tracks for no gain. Gary Collins punted to Willie Wood on the Green Bay 25 for no return.

With 11:05 left in the half, Starr handed off to Hornung who picked up just two yards in a sweep to the left. Starr overthrew his next pass to Dowler, but on the next play he connected with Dowler for 12 yards and a first down. Starr hit Dowler again for six yards. With the ball on the Green Bay 45, Hornung took the handoff for a yard to the right. He tried the left side on the next play, but the Golden Boy got nothing. Chandler came in to punt the ball. Kelly caught it for a fair catch on the Cleveland 15.

Ryan's pass on first down was aimed at Warfield, but Jeter broke up the play. Brown got nothing on second down. Ryan passed again on third down, but Wood grabbed it on the Browns 25 and returned the ball 15 yards to the Cleveland 10.

On first down, the Packers were penalized five yards for an illegal motion. With the ball on the 15 now, Starr's pass into the end zone to Dale failed. Starr passed to Taylor in the flat, but the Cajun missed it. One more try from the 15 to Dowler on five came up nil. In came the kicking team again, and Chandler added three points to raise the score to 13-9 in favor of the Packers.

Chandler kicked off again, this time to Walter Roberts on the four-yard line. The Cleveland receiver returned the ball to the Browns 31, but a clipping penalty took the ball back to the 16. Brown gained nine yards. Green got nothing on second down. Then Brown picked up 14 yards for a first down to the 39. Ryan's pass to Warfield went incomplete. Brown went left for eight yards, but on his next carry he lost a yard when Tom Brown came through for the Packers. Collins punted again with the ball going out of bounds on the GB four.

On first down, Taylor bulled his way through the left side for four yards. He followed that with three yards to the right. Then bad news when Starr's pass was intercepted by Walter Beach on the Pack's 30-yard line.

Ryan's first down pass to Collins went incomplete at the goal line. Dave Robinson and Ray Nitschke sacked Ryan for a five-yard loss. Ryan then found Brown for 14 yards, a yard short of a first down. Groza kicked a 28-yard field goal with 48 seconds remaining in the half to make the score, 13-12, Packers. Groza kicked off, and Tom Moore caught the ball on the Cleveland seven and returned it to the Green Bay 32. Taylor ran for two yards, then Lombardi let the clock run out.

Chandler kicked off to start the second half. Roberts caught the ball four yards deep into the end zone and returned the kick 35 yards to the Cleveland 31. On the first play from scrimmage, Ron Kostelnik threw Brown for a two-yard loss. Bob Jeter stopped Green on the next play for no gain. Ryan then connected with Collins for 17 yards and a first down at the Browns 46. Ryan's next pass was aimed at Warfield but went incomplete. He tried hitting Brown next, but that one also went for nought. On third down, Lionel Aldridge nailed Ryan for a loss of eight yards, forcing another punt by Collins. Pitts fielded the ball on the Green Bay 20 and lost 10 yards on the return.

Hornung took a handoff from Starr and picked up five yards through the left side. The Golden Boy took another turn with the ball and gained four yards into the right side. Taylor got his turn and burst through the right side for two yards and a first down. From the 21, the Cajun ripped off five more yards. Then Starr found Dowler over the middle for 12 yards and another first down. Taylor charged through the left side for eight yards and followed that with the same play for seven yards and another first down. With the ball now on the Browns 45, Starr passed to Taylor for 10 yards and another first down on the 35. Hornung got the ball again and busted through the left side for 20 yards and a first down on the Cleveland 15. The Cajun then went up the middle for two yards. With less than six minutes left in the quarter, Starr pitched to Hornung and he followed a convoy into the end zone for a touchdown. Chandler was perfect with the PAT, and the Packers were now ahead, 20-12. Green Bay ate up six minutes and 33 seconds off the clock with their scoring drive.

Roberts took Chandler's kickoff two yards into the end zone and returned it to the Cleveland 31. Ryan dropped back to pass but was forced to run with ball, gaining eight yards up the middle of his line. The Packers were called for a face masking penalty that added 15 yards to the play. With first and 10 on the Green Bay 46, Brown bulled through the left side for eight yards. He followed that with a three-yard burst and a first down. Ryan passed to Collins for seven yards. He tried to hit Brown in the end zone, but Nitschke fouled up the play. Willie Davis and Lionel Aldridge sacked Ryan for a two-yard loss. With the ball on the GB 30, Collier sent in his kicking team. Groza got the kick away, but Henry Jordan tipped it and the ball fell dead in the end zone.

First and 10 on Pack's own 20.

Starr started the possession with a pass to Anderson over the middle, but the ball missed its target. On second down, Starr found Dale for 13 yards and a first down. With another first down, Taylor took the handoff and bulldozed through the center line for four yards. Starr called the same play, and Taylor hammered his way for six more yards and another first down. The gun sounded the end of the third quarter.

On the first play in the fourth quarter, Hornung took the pitch from Starr, faded to the right, threw an option pass to Dale, but it fell incomplete. Starr found Dowler over middle and hit him with an 18-yard gainer and another first down. Once again, the Packers appeared to be on another scoring march. The Cajun took another handoff from Starr and bulled through the left side for three yards. Next play Taylor charged up the middle for six yards. On third down, Taylor tried the middle again but only managed to gain two yards. Even so, that was enough for another first down on the Browns 27. On his fourth consecutive play, Taylor picked up five yards to the 22. Hornung tried the right side and got only one yard. Next play he tried the left side and was stopped cold. Lombardi sent in the kicking team. Chandler booted his third field goal of the game, raising the lead to 23-12 with 9:28 left on the clock.

Leroy Kelly caught the kickoff on his own seven, that raced 40 yards to the Packers 47. Ryan's first down pass was aimed at Collins, but it failed. He connected with Brown on second down, but the Pack defense stopped him at the line of scrimmage. With third and 10 yet, Ryan dropped back to pass again, but Davis had other thoughts and nailed the Cleveland QB for a five-yard loss. Collins punted again, and the Packers let the ball roll dead on their own seven.

With 7:40 left in the game, Lombardi chose to have his team eat clock. Taylor lost two yards, then Starr was sacked for three more backwards. Taylor gained back the five yards on the next play. Then in came Chandler to punt the ball again. He got it away, but the Cleveland rushers roughed him for a 15-yard penalty and an automatic first down on Green Bay's 22. Hornung gained eight yards. Taylor five. Another first down. Hornung stopped for no gain. Taylor stopped for no gain. Taylor picked up three. Chandler punted again to Roberts who caught the ball on his team's 17. He returned it for 10 yards.

On first down, Herb Adderley snared Ryan's pass on the Pack's 25-yard line.

Three plays later the game was over.

Packers 23, Browns 12.

The Green Bay Packers were NFL Champions for the third time in five seasons.

§ § §

Summary

I'll let that great sportswriter, Packers' historian, and most excellent gentleman, the late Lee Remmel, sum up the Packers title game win:

As Green Bay's soggy, begrimed world champions clumped through the long gray tunnel to their Lambeau Field dressing room Sunday afternoon, an exuberant Elijah Pitts whooped,

"We is the greatest!"

Ex-pedagogue Vince Lombardi, who didn't hear the ebullient declaration, might have taken issue with Elijah's grammar, but he heartily endorsed the sentiment minutes later.

Encircled by a crush of newsmen in his functional first floor office," where he presented a picture of restrained jubilation, the Packers' square cut headmaster asserted with evident pride,

> ***"This team has more character than any other team I've had. And I think that is a great compliment to them. I think I marked this team pretty well (during the training season). I said this may not be the best team I've had, but it has the most character.***
>
> ***I think it's got a mark to it. It's got a great deal of perseverance. It never seemed to count itself out. A lot of things happened to us this season, but the players closed their mouths and never said a word to the press or anyone. They kept their mouths shut.***

> ***Everything that was said was said here (in the locker room). I'm talking about injuries and a number of things."***

This prompted an allusion to the Pack's mid-season recession, which Lombardi acknowledged.

> ***"That's what I said. A lot of teams would have folded, but we stayed right in there. We had a break, however. Let's not say we won it all by ourselves. We had a break from the Bears (the Bruins' 13-0 victory over the Colts in Baltimore Dec. 5).***

Someone interjected,

> ***"That's what Halas said the day the Packers beat them here in October, that he was going to give you some help along the way."***

Lombardi smiled.

> ***"I'm glad he said that."***

The Pack's guiding genius earlier had indicated the manner in which the victory had been accomplished, noting with a twinkle,

> ***"Maybe some of the people who say we don't have any offense will change their minds now."***

One eager scribe observed,

> ***"You predicted this last summer." Winning the title, he meant.***

> ***"I don't think I did that,"***

chuckled Lombardi,

> ***"but it sounds good."***

Another reporter asked if he had decided to play fundamental football because of the field condition. Vince replied.

> ***"Yes, we did, but we're a basic football team anyway. The Browns' attack also had dictated the same approach. I think you have to control the ball to beat the Browns because they have a great offense."***

Had he made any changes in pre-game planning?

> ***"No, I didn't. That's what you get out of when you are a basic football team. I am glad people believe that, anyway. We knew by Wednesday what we were going to try to do."***

Lombardi was asked why he replaced Doug Hart with Bob Jeter at right cornerback in the first quarter.

> ***"We thought Jeter would do a better job of covering Paul Warfield. Jeter is probably the fastest man we have on the squad—Jeter and Long."***

Quizzed about the Browns early success with the pass, Vince observed,

> ***"We didn't react as well as we might have. But let's not take anything away from them—they were beautiful passes. That one to Collins in the corner of end zone was a beautifully thrown ball."***

Commenting on the Packers' quarterback play, Lombardi declared,

> ***"I think Starr was really sharp. I think he called a great game. It was not the best day for passing, of course. The receivers couldn't make their cuts well and the ball was slick. I***

think you could see that with Ryan a couple of times."

Taylor and Hornung somebody suggested, hadn't looked too bad, considering they were supposed to be in the twilight of their careers. Appreciating the understatement, Lombardi responded with one of his own. He chuckled,

"I think there's a little spark left in them."

In the dressing room proper, all was confusion. Television cameras and wires, plus news photographers and swarms of reporters from throughout the nation crammed every cubic inch of the Packers' plush green and gold quarters, clambering over each other on an attempt to pry comments from the heroes of Green Bay's ninth world title.

Before greeting the press, Lombardi had taken note of the invasion, particularly the electronic aspect. Still wearing bespattered rain gear, he took time out from his preparations for the TV eye' to admonish his athletes,

"Watch your language now."

Elsewhere, rookie Junior Coffey was shouting to no one in particular,

"How sweet it is!"

In another corner of the bedlam, Defense Coach Phil Bengtson was embracing one of his proteges Willie Davis.

At the other end of the Pack's palatial quarters, prime hero Jim Taylor was almost inaccessible. His rugged features still caked with mud, the Bayou Bronco patiently held forth for wave after wave of newsmen, who delayed departure for the shower room for more than an hour.

Wending his way through the mass of humanity, Lombardi finally managed to reach his multi-muscled fullback.

"Let me shake your hand again. You did a great job, a great job. And I know you were hurt, too."

Taylor smiled as the Packer coach departed.

Lombardi went back to the sanctum of his office. A smile of satisfaction spread across his face. His boys had won his third National Football League Championship in six years, seven years, if you count his first season as a head coach.

General Manager Vince Lombardi nodded and sat down at his desk. He picked up the list of draftees. His head bobbed with a slight grin. Then he dropped the list and picked up two signed contracts. An even broader smile spread over his face as he whispered to himself.

"Grabowski. Anderson."

§ § §

About Larry Names

The day I met John Torinus, Sr., was the day I began focusing on the fascinating history of the Green Bay Packers."

John's first-hand stories about the Packers sparked Names into digging deep into researching the history of the most unique sports franchise in the world. He has made it his mission to separate fact from fiction and tell the real story of the history of the Green Bay Packers.

Larry Names has had 45 titles published to date, 28 novels, and the remainder non-fiction all dealing with sports teams or sports figures. He is a recognized authority on the Green Bay Packers, Chicago Cubs and Chicago White Sox.

He resides in Wisconsin with his wife Peg. They have a son, Torry and a daughter, Tegan.

Larry has four children from his first marriage: daughter Sigrid, an author in her own rite; son Paul; daughter Kristin, an award-winning screenwriter; and daughter Sonje. He also has 18 grandchildren and two great-grandchildren.

The author was born in Mishawaka, Indiana and has lived in nine different states during his life and attended 11 schools growing up plus three colleges after serving his country in the Navy. He is an avid researcher, genealogist, traveler, and collector of memories and coins.

For more information about Larry Names and his books, go to www.larrynames.com

"Like" Larry Names on his Facebook Fan page at: https://www.facebook.com/LarryNames/

♦♦♦

BIBLIOGRAPHY

Books

The Baseball Encyclopedia, Sixth Edition, Revised, Updated & Expanded, edited by Joseph L. Reichler, Macmillan Publishing Co., Inc., 1985

George Halas and the Chicago Bears, George Vass, Henry Regnery Company, 1971

The Green Bay Packers, Pro Football's Pioneer Team, Chuck Johnson, Thomas Nelson & Sons, 1961.

The Green Bay Packers, The Story of Professional Football, Arch Ward, G.P. Putnam's Sons, 1946.

Halas on Halas, George Halas with Gwen Morgan, and Arthur Veysey, McGraw-Hill Book Co., 1979

History of American Football, Allison Danzig, Prentice-Hall, Inc., 1956.

The NFL's Official Encyclopedic History of Professional Football, Macmillan Publishing Co., Inc., 1973

Official 1985 National Football League Record & Fact Book.

The Packer Legend: An Inside Look, John B. Torinus, Sr., Laranmark Press, 1982

This Day In Packer History, Jeff Everson, Angel Press of WI, 1998

The Pro Football Digest, edited by Robert Billings, Digest Books, Inc., 1978

The Scrapbook History of Pro Football, Richard M. Cohen, Jordan A. Deutsch, Roland T. Johnson, and David S. Neft, The Bobbs-Merrill Company, 1977.

VINCE, A Personal Biography of Vince Lombardi, Michael O'Brien, Quill, 1987

Lombardi: His Life and Times, Robert Wells. Wisconsin House, LTD, 1971

Lombardi: Winning Is the Only Thing, Jerry Kramer, World Publishing Co., 1970

NEWSPAPERS

Chicago Sun, The
Chicago Daily News, The
Chicago Herald-Examiner, The
Chicago Tribune, The
Daily Georgian and Sunday American
Green Bay Gazette
Green Bay Press-Gazette, The
Iron Mountain News, The
The Los Angeles Examiner, The
Los Angeles Times, The
Milwaukee Journal, The
Milwaukee Sentinel, The
New York Daily News, The
New York Times, The
Packer Report, The
The South Bend Tribune, The

PERIODICALS

Collier's
Time
Sport Magazine
Sports Illustrated
Touchback, The
Look

Green Bay Packers Media Guide, 1986 Green Bay Packers Media Guide, 1987 Green Bay Packers Media Guide, 1988 Green Bay Packers Media Guide, 1989 Green Bay Packers Media Guide, 1990 Green Bay Packers Media Guide, 1991 Green Bay Packers Media Guide, 1992 Green Bay Packers Media Guide, 1993 Green Bay Packers Media Guide, 1994 Green Bay Packers Yearbook.

§§§

LARRY NAMES

Book List

NON-FICTION

LAMBEAU YEARS, THE, PART ONE, THE HISTORY OF THE GREEN BAY PACKERS, VOL. 1

LAMBEAU YEARS, THE, PART TWO, THE HISTORY OF THE GREEN BAY PACKERS, VOL. 2

LAMBEAU YEARS THE, PART THREE, THE HISTORY OF THE GREEN BAY PACKERS, VOL. 3

SHAMEFUL YEARS, THE, THE HISTORY OF THE GREEN BAY PACKERS, VOL. 4

LOMBARDI'S DESTINY, PART ONE, THE HISTORY OF THE GREEN BAY PACKERS, VOL. 5

GREEN BAY PACKERS FACTS & TRIVIA, 1ST EDITION

GREEN BAY PACKERS FACTS & TRIVIA, 2ND EDITION

GREEN BAY PACKERS FACTS & TRIVIA, 3RD EDITION

GREEN BAY PACKERS FACTS & TRIVIA, 4TH EDITION

BURY MY HEART AT WRIGLEY FIELD: THE HISTORY OF THE CHICAGO CUBS

-WHEN THE CUBS WERE THE WHITE STOCKINGS, PART ONE

CHICAGO WHITE SOX FACTS & TRIVIA

OUT AT HOME BY MILT PAPPAS, WAYNE MAUSSER AND LARRY NAMES

HOME PLATE BY STEVE TROUT, DAVE CAMPBELL, AND LARRY NAMES

DEAR PETE: THE LIFE OF PETE ROSE

FICTION

SHAMAN'S SECRET, THE

LEGEND OF EAGLE CLAW, THE

BOSE

BOOMTOWN

COWBOY CONSPIRACY

PROSPECTING FOR MURDER

TWICE DEAD

THE OSWALD REFLECTION

IRONCLADS: MAN-OF-WAR

IRONCLADS: TIDES-OF-WAR

TEGAN O'MALLEY – THE TRAVELER IN TIME

TEGAN O'MALLEY – STOWAWAY ON TITANIC

Maisy-A TWO REEL MURDER – STARRING MACK SENNETT & MABEL NORMAND – A MAISY MALONE MYSTERY--BOOK 1**Maisy**-MURDER ON RATTLESNAKE ISLAND: STARRING MACK SENNETT AND MABEL NORMAND (A MAISY MALONE MYSTERY BOOK 2)

Maisy-MURDER IN THE FIRST REEL: STARRING MABEL NORMAND AND CHARLES CHAPLIN-A Maisy Malone Mystery BOOK 3

Maisy-MURDER ON THE CUTTING ROOM FLOOR: STARRING MABEL NORMAND AND ROSCOE ARBUCKLE-A MAISY MALONE MYSTERY BOOK 4

Maisy-MURDER IS NO LAUGHING MATTER: STARRING Roscoe ARBUCKLE AND MINTA DURFEE-A MAISY MALONE MYSTERY BOOK 5

With others

HUNTER'S ORANGE

PK FACTOR, THE

As Bryce Harte/Larry Names

CREED #1: CREED/A TEXAS CREED

CREED #2: WANTED/TEXAS PAYBACK

CREED #3: POWDERKEG/TEXAS POWDERKEG

CREED #4: CREED'S WAR/KENTUCKY PRIDE

CREED #5: MISSOURI GUNS

CREED #6: TEXAN'S HONOR

CREED #7: BETRAYED/TEXAS FREEDOM

CREED #8: COLORADO PREY

CREED #9: CHEYENNE JUSTICE

CREED #10: ARKANSAS RAIDERS

CREED #11: BOSTON MOUNTAIN RENEGADES

AUDIOBOOKS

CREED #1: SLATER CREED, THE

CREED #2: TEXAS PAYBACK

CREED #3: POWDERKEG

CREED #4: KENTUCKY PRIDE

CREED #5: MISSOURI GUNS

CREED #6: TEXAN'S HONOR

CREED #7: TEXAS FREEDOM

CREED #8: COLORADO PREY

CREED #9: CHEYENNE JUSTICE

CREED #10: ARKANSAS RAIDERS

CREED #11: BOSTON MOUNTAIN RENEGADES

IRONCLADS: THE TIDES OF WAR

Maisy-A TWO REEL MURDER – STARRING MACK SENNETT & MABEL NORMAND – A MAISY MALONE MYSTERY BOOK 1

Maisy-MURDER ON RATTLESNAKE ISLAND: STARRING MACK SENNETT AND MABEL NORMAND (A MAISY MALONE MYSTERY BOOK 2)

Maisy-MURDER IN THE FIRST REEL: STARRING MABEL NORMAND AND CHARLES CHAPLIN-A Maisy Malone Mystery BOOK 3

Maisy-MURDER ON THE CUTTING ROOM FLOOR: STARRING MABEL NORMAND AND ROSCOE ARBUCKLE-A MAISY MALONE MYSTERY BOOK 4

Maisy-MURDER IS NO LAUGHING MATTER: STARRING Roscoe ARBUCKLE AND MINTA DURFEE-A MAISY MALONE MYSTERY BOOK 5

OSWALD REFLECTION, THE

PROSPECTING FOR MURDER
SHAMAN'S SECRET, THE
BOSE
BOOMTOWN

KINDLE EDITIONS
THE OSWALD REFLECTION

BURY MY HEART AT WRIGLEY FIELD: THE HISTORY OF THE CHICAGO CUBS

-WHEN THE CUBS WERE THE WHITE STOCKINGS, PART ONE

PROSPECTING FOR MURDER

TEGAN O'MALLEY – THE TRAVELER IN TIME

TEGAN O'MALLEY – STOWAWAY ON TITANIC

IRONCLADS: TIDES OF WAR

CREED #1: A TEXAS CREED

CREED #2: TEXAS PAYBACK

CREED #3: TEXAS POWDERKEG

CREED #4: KENTUCKY PRIDE

CREED #5: MISSOURI GUNS

CREED #6: TEXAN'S HONOR

CREED #7: TEXAS FREEDOM

CREED #8: COLORADO PREY

CREED #9: CHEYENNE JUSTICE

CREED #10: ARKANSAS RAIDERS

CREED #11: BOSTON MOUNTAIN RENAGES

LAMBEAU YEARS, THE, PART ONE, THE HISTORY OF THE GREEN BAY PACKERS, VOL. 1

LAMBEAU YEARS, THE, PART TWO, THE HISTORY OF THE GREEN BAY PACKERS, VOL. 2

LAMBEAU YEARS THE, PART THREE, THE HISTORY OF THE GREEN BAY PACKERS, VOL. 3

SHAMEFUL YEARS. THE, THE HISTORY OF THE GREEN BAY PACKERS, VOL. 4

LOMBARDI'S DESTINY, PART ONE, THE HISTORY OF THE GREEN BAY PACKERS, VOL. 5

OMBARDI'S DESTINY, PART TWO, THE HISTORY OF THE GREEN BAY PACKERS, VOL. 6

LOMBARDI'S DESTINY, PART THREE, THE HISTORY OF THE GREEN BAY PACKERS, VOL. 7

Maisy-A TWO REEL MURDER – STARRING MACK SENNETT & MABEL NORMAND – A MAISY MALONE MYSTERY BOOK 1

Maisy-MURDER ON RATTLESNAKE ISLAND: STARRING MACK SENNETT AND MABEL NORMAND (A MAISY MALONE MYSTERY BOOK 2)

Maisy-MURDER IN THE FIRST REEL: STARRING MABEL NORMAND AND CHARLES CHAPLIN-A Maisy Malone Mystery BOOK 3

Maisy-MURDER ON THE CUTTING ROOM FLOOR: STARRING MABEL NORMAND AND ROSCOE ARBUCKLE-A MAISY MALONE MYSTERY BOOK 4

Maisy-MURDER IS NO LAUGHING MATTER: STARRING Roscoe ARBUCKLE AND MINTA DURFEE-A MAISY MALONE MYSTERY BOOK 5

§ § §

INDEX

www.ingramcontent.com/pod-product-compliance
Lightning Source LLC
Chambersburg PA
CBHW060019100426
42740CB00010B/1530
9780910937900